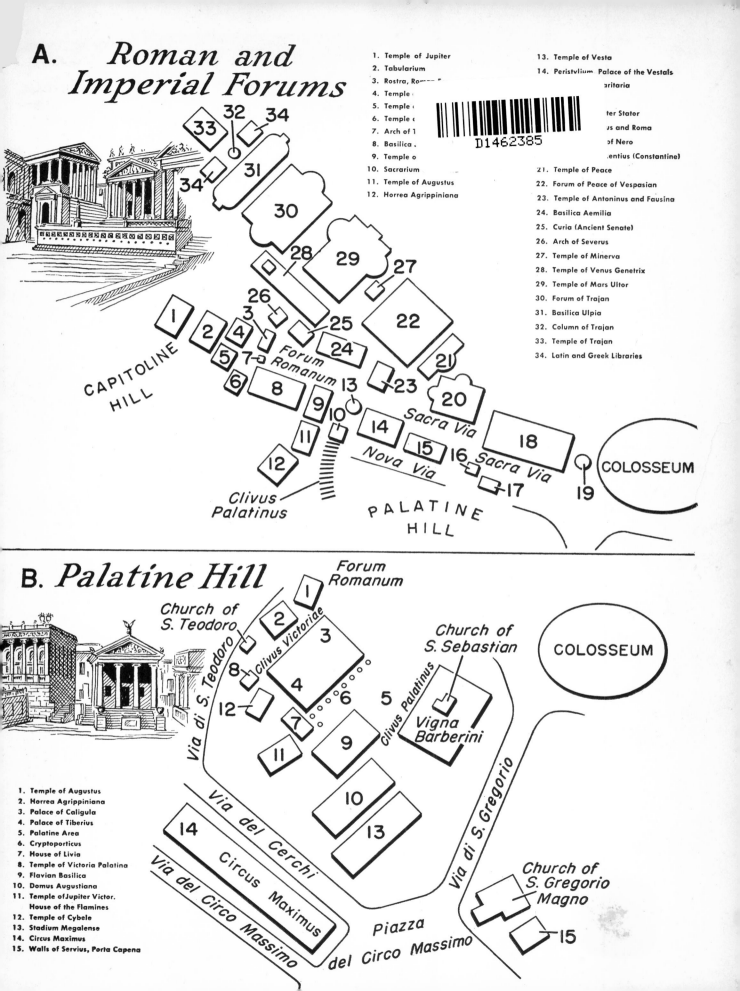

A. Roman and Imperial Forums

1. Temple of Jupiter
2. Tabularium
3. Rostra, Roman
4. Temple
5. Temple
6. Temple
7. Arch of 1
8. Basilica
9. Temple o
10. Sacrarium
11. Temple of Augustus
12. Horrea Agrippiniana

13. Temple of Vesta
14. Peristylium Palace of the Vestals
   aritaria

   ter Stator
   us and Roma
   of Nero
   entius (Constantine)
21. Temple of Peace
22. Forum of Peace of Vespasian
23. Temple of Antoninus and Fausina
24. Basilica Aemilia
25. Curia (Ancient Senate)
26. Arch of Severus
27. Temple of Minerva
28. Temple of Venus Genetrix
29. Temple of Mars Ultor
30. Forum of Trajan
31. Basilica Ulpia
32. Column of Trajan
33. Temple of Trajan
34. Latin and Greek Libraries

CAPITOLINE HILL

Forum Romanum

Sacra Via

Nova Via

Clivus Palatinus

PALATINE HILL

COLOSSEUM

B. Palatine Hill

Forum Romanum

Church of S. Teodoro

Clivus Victoriae

Via di S. Teodoro

Church of S. Sebastian

Clivus Palatinus

Vigna Barberini

COLOSSEUM

Via di S. Gregorio

Via del Cerchi

Circus Maximus

Via del Circo Massimo

Piazza del Circo Massimo

Church of S. Gregorio Magno

1. Temple of Augustus
2. Horrea Agrippiniana
3. Palace of Caligula
4. Palace of Tiberius
5. Palatine Area
6. Cryptoporticus
7. House of Livia
8. Temple of Victoria Palatina
9. Flavian Basilica
10. Domus Augustiana
11. Temple of Jupiter Victor. House of the Flamines
12. Temple of Cybele
13. Stadium Megalense
14. Circus Maximus
15. Walls of Servius, Porta Capena

THE GRANDEUR THAT WAS

ROME

THE GRANDEUR

The amazing monuments of
Imperial Rome, today for
the most part in ruins,
stir the imagination to
leap barriers of time and
recreate the splendors of
the capital of the ancient
world—its forums, temples
palaces, theaters, mausoleums
and huge arenas where
charioteers contended for
the palm of victory and
Christians were martyred.
These Restorations give
concrete and striking form
to the phantoms of the past
evoked by the surviving
fragments of a grandiose
civilization.

THAT WAS

ROME

BY

Giuseppe Gatteschi

EDITED BY

Dr. G. Nicotra Di Leopoldo

HASTINGS HOUSE, PUBLISHERS, NEW YORK

T HE VISITOR TO ROME, when he pauses to contemplate the ancient ruins scattered throughout the city, cannot achieve complete esthetic enjoyment of those fragments of the past because he is continually wondering what the buildings of which they are the surviving relics really looked like. He listens eagerly to the *cicerone,* but the latter talks much yet says little, because he has neither the ability nor the qualifications to evoke a vision of the ancient architectural glories that once distinguished the city.

The discerning reader will obtain a vivid impression of Imperial Rome from the Restorations of ancient buildings and monuments shown in this book, and this pleasant archeological excursion will help him to a realization of the scope and splendor of a civilization that in some respects achieved the loftiest forms of human expression. He will experience the unusual and unforgettable emotion of having actually lived in a strange, a fantastically strange city of another era and world. He will come out of this dream richer by a treasure-trove of artistic and historical knowledge far exceeding his most extravagant expectations.

Giuseppe Gatteschi was born in Florence in 1862. His first venture into archaeology was in connection with interesting researches in the Egyptian field. But he soon succumbed to the fascination of the grandeur of Imperial Rome and turned his efforts to reconstruction of the amazing monuments of the Eternal City. He labored unceasingly for upward of thirty-four years on researches connected with Roman ruins. I well remember that strange room in which he worked, with its walls lined completely with files filled with autograph letters from eminent personages praising his wonderful undertaking. He was also a fine musical amateur, and devoted a corner of his studio to his library of composers which included the works of Puccini, Leoncavallo, Boito, Massenet and others, all of whom had written him enthusiastic letters which he filed with those of the greatest archaeologists of Europe. He was a member of the Archaeological Committee of Rome, and wrote many interesting and authoritative articles about his discoveries for various professional periodicals in Italy and elsewhere. He was ever an idealist, an enthusiast;

5

it did not matter to him that society never gave him the material rewards he was entitled to for his eminent achievemens. The labor he devoted to creating the wonderful Restorations collected in this volume was enormous. I would like to quote from a letter written him by the Minister of Public Instruction and Beaux Arts of Paris in this connection:

"Dear Mr. Gatteschi: I was deeply moved and filled with wonder by your very kind despatch to me of the package containing your Restorations of Rome, which you have been good enough to let me see, and for which I am not sufficiently able to express the gratitude I feel.

"I have examined your beautiful resurrection of these antiquities with great interest and admiration, and I realize even at this distance the scientific knowledge, the acumen, the tremendous labor you had to apply to produce this work of which you may well be proud. Please accept my warmest congratulations.

"V. Leclerc. Architect of the Government
Former Member of the Academy of France at Rome"

In addition to the Restorations of Imperial Rome, Professor Gatteschi was busy with another very important undertaking prior to his death, *A History of Theaters from the Earliest Times Down to the Present Day*. He showed me some very interesting material covering this subject, and some letters in praise of his project, especially one from M. Garnier, the famous architect of the Paris Opera, and others from Bernard Shaw and Luigi Pirandello, the great Italian playright.

The Restorations collected in this volume are based on the authority of the Classics, on reproductions of ancient buildings upon ancient coins and bas-reliefs, on traditions and the map of Severus, *(Forma Urbis Romae)* discovered in the Roman Forum. Finally, to complete his researches, Professor Gatteschi had engaged in a meticulous study of the work of the most celebrated architects of the 16th century, who depicted or described ancient buildings still surviving in their day but which have disappeared since then, and of the discoveries resulting from excavations made during the period from 1896 to 1923. Actually he carried these studies down through the discoveries of 1924, measuring, calculating, checking each monument with greatest care for accuracy, always with an infinite love for these classic ruins of the Eternal City.

The last time I saw him—in February 1935 (he died in March of that year)— he was very ill; he lay there, at death's door, but indomitable in his will to work on, surrounded by his books and material upon which he had spent so many nights in ardent research and labor.

G. NICOTRA DI LEOPOLDO

Following are a few appreciations, by outstanding authorities, of Professor Gatteschi's Restorations.

From Cardinal Pietro Maffi, Archbishop of Pisa:

Your archaeological Album will certainly meet with the approbation and the praise of everybody. I am eager, and wish with all my heart, that a publication of such a great interest may see the light soon. So many treasures will be disclosed to the general knowledge and will prove of extraordinary value; these treasures have been till now accessible to only a privileged few. *Pisa, July 10, 1925*

From Gabriele D'Annunzio:

Your work endows with a new life the documents of the Latin classics. *Vittoriale, 1927*

Some of the greatest authorities on the Topography of old Rome write as follows.

From Professor Dr. Christian Huelsen of the Imperial Institute of Archaeology:

. . . The method of comparing each Restoration to the actual conditions of the ruins today is a very good one and is calculated to give us the best idea of the beauty of Imperial Rome, as shown by the most recent discoveries of Roman archaeology. The artistic execution is excellent; and I compliment you on having done a work so useful not only to scholars of Roman topography and architecture, but also to everybody who wishes to admire Rome by understanding the inner beauty of the Eternal City. *Rome, March 19, 1910*

Senator Professor Rodolfo Lanciani, Chairman of Roman Topography at the University of Rome:

. . . Work of great archaeological value, very important to the students of Roman topography and archaeology. *Rome, November 16, 1910*

From Comm. Orazio Marucchi, Professor of Christian Archaeology at the University of Rome:

The Restorations of Imperial Rome by the archaeologist Prof. Giuseppe Gatteschi have been carried out with such care and competence, based on historical sources, as to constitute a real treasure for the scholars and amateurs of the beauty of ancient Rome. *Rome, April 10, 1919*

THE TOUR STARTS with the Capitoline Hill on which were perched the magnificent Temple of Jupiter and, nearby, other notable monuments. From the Capitoline Hill the tourist will descend to the Roman Forum where every stone recalls the grandeur that was Rome. At this point he may visit the Forum of Augustus whose ruins are located in the vicinity. From the Roman Forum he will proceed to the Temple of Venus and Rome, at the eastern end of the Forum. One of the apses, the eastern one, faced toward the Colosseum.

From the Roman Forum the sightseer will climb the Palatine Hill, today covered for the most part with ruins, but in Imperial times crowded with dazzling palaces and temples and monuments. Then he will descend again, this time to the Circus Maximus at the southern base of the hill, the greatest outdoor sports arena ever constructed by man, and from there, along the modern Via del Cerchi to the Piazza d. Circo Massimo near which stood the ancient Porta Capena, starting point of the Appian Way, queen of Roman long-distance thruways. From there the tour turns back, paralleling the Tiber, to the Forum Boarium, ancient cattle market, and to the remains of the Theater of Marcellus on which now is perched the Orsini Palace; nearby is the site of the Portico of Octavia, named for Augustus' sister, who was spurned by Anthony because of his infatuation for Cleopatra, and also but a stone's throw away is the Island of the Tiber, where stood in ancient days the Temple of Aesculapius.

This is probably sufficient for the first day. Indeed, it would be advisable to split this part of the tour into two days of sightseeing.

On the third day, the tourist had better start with the Nymphaeum of Alexander, whose ruins are still to be seen in the Vittorio Emanuele Gardens at the Esquiline Hill; then he will take the Via Nazionale to Trajan's Forum, which in its day was perhaps the most imposing of all the Imperial Forums, and then will continue to the Piazza Venezia, and to the Corso Vittorio Emanuele. On the first block facing the Corso was the center of the ancient Egyptian sanctuary; the tourist will be interested to compare the present-day buildings on this site with the amazing structures shown in the Restorations.

Only a short distance northwest is the Pantheon, one of the few ancient buildings of Rome preserved nearly intact. Proceeding westward on the Corso Vittorio Emanuele, in the direction of the Tiber, the tourist will soon come to the Largo Argentina, near which he will observe the important excavations of 1926-1931; the Restorations recreate the buildings that once stood here: the Temple of Minerva Chalcidica, the round Temple of Hercules Custos and the Curia of Pompey where Julius Caesar was assassinated.

Now proceed westward to Piazza Campo dei Fiori where the grandiose Theater of Pompey and the Temple of Venus once loomed and near which were the extensive Porticoes of Pompey.

From the Corso Vittorio Emanuele the sightseer should now take the Via del Corso northward till he arrives at the Piazza Augusto Imperatore, where he will behold with amazement the vast ruins near the Tiber of the Mausoleum of Augustus, the grandeur of which is shown in the Restoration. To the southwestward, on the other side of the river, he will see the Castel S. Angelo, all that remains of the magnificent Tomb of Hadrian. From the Castel S. Angelo he will proceed westward to St. Peter in Vaticano, the greatest church in Christendom. Here once stood the huge Circus of Nero where St. Peter met a martyr's death.

Following this itinerary, with the Restorations in his hand, the tourist will be able to get an impressive picture of the vanished grandeur of Imperial Rome.

THE GRANDEUR THAT WAS

ROME

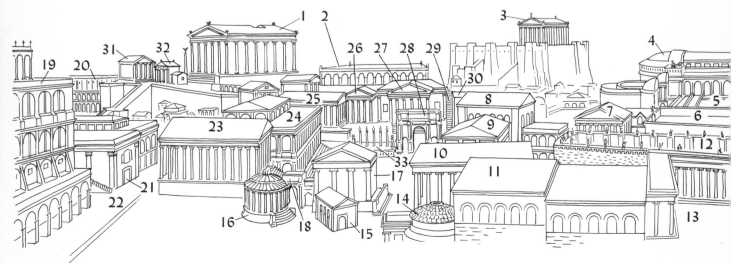

GENERAL PANORAMA IN IMPERIAL TIMES

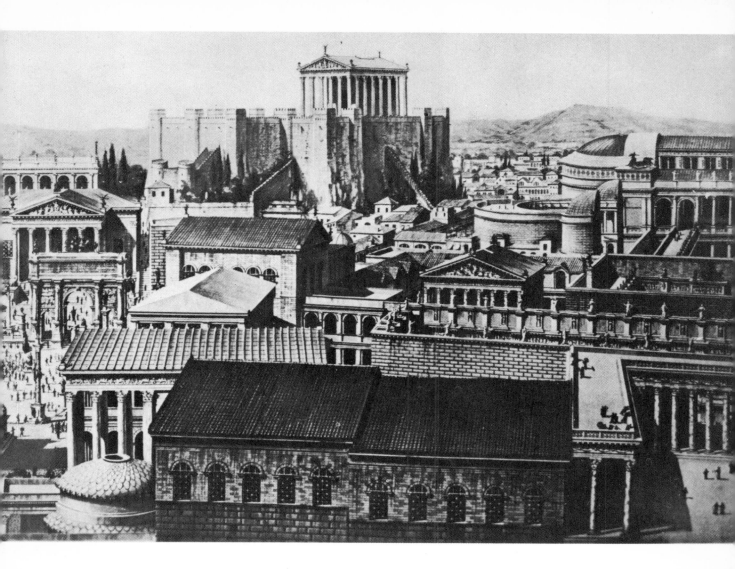

1. Temple of Jupiter
2. Tablinarium
3. Temple of Minerva
4. Basilica Ulpia in Trajan's Forum
5. Forum of Trajan
6. Forum of Augustus
7. Temple of Venus Genetrix in Julius Caesar's Forum
8. Curia (Roman Senate)
9. Basilica Aemilia
10. Temple of Antonius and Faustina
11. Templum Sacrae Urbis (Archives of the City)
12. Forum of Nerva
13. Forum of Peace
14. Temple of Romulus, son of Maxentius
15. The Regia
16. Temple of Vesta

17. Temple of Caesar
18. Arch of Augustus
19. Palace of Caligula
20. Theater of Marcellus
21. House of the Vestals
22. Nova Via
23. Temple of Castor and Pollux
24. Basilica Julia
25. Temple of Saturn
26. Temple of Vespasian
27. Temple of Concord
28. Arch of Alexander Severus
29. Scalae Gemoniae (Stairway to Capitoline Hill)
30. Carcer (Prison)
31. Temple of Faith
32. Augusteum
33. Rostra in the Roman Forum

13

CONTEMPORARY GENERAL PANORAMA

THE RESTORATION SHOWS A panorama of the Capitoline Hill (Monte Cȧpi-
tolino), the Forum Romanum, and the temples and monuments of the vicinity. The
View of the Present-day Site shows, by contrast, the ruins of the Monte Capitolino,
the Roman Forum, the Palace of Caligula, etc. These edifices are described in de-
tail and shown in the Restorations, that follow.

14   In the panorama of the View of the Present-day Site you see the astounding
surviving relics of the great past, ruins to be computed in terms of time and men.
Here you have the Church of Aracoeli and the Monument of Victor Emanuel
which have replaced the Citadel (at the northern end of the Capitoline Hill),

ancient and glorious fortress of the city, and the Temple of Juno Moneta; the modern Campidoglio which has replaced the ancient *Tabularium;* the former Caffarelli Palace built on the site of the majestic Temple of Jupiter; the obscure ruins of the Palace of Caligula; the marbles of the Basilica Julia and the House of the Vestals, with three lonely surviving columns of the Temple of Castor and Pollux; the sight of all this is like a dagger aimed at one's heart. What desolation man has caused in less than 14 centuries! Happy he who can really know the beauty of this vanished world and make it live again in his imagination. He may walk in pride, rejoicing in this noble and exalted intellectual adventure.

15

THE TEMPLE OF JUPITER CAPITOLINUS, the ancient *Capitolium* (Capitol) was located in the area of the old Caffarelli Palace with its gardens and stables, all the way to the Via di Monte Caprino.

When the foundations of the building were laid, in 533 B.C., the Augurs, addressing the envoys of the last Roman King Tarquinius Superbus, made the following prophecy: "Oh, Romans! Go and make it known that the place where you have found the skull (head) is destined to become the capital of all Italy." From that time on the place was called Capitolinus (from *caput* meaning head).

The Capitolium became the august center of Roman paganism. After many vicissitudes, including a conflagration during the troubled times of Vitellius, it was splendidly rebuilt by the Emperor Domitian in 82 A.D.

The pavement of the temple, uncovered in 1919, is about 203½ feet long and about 187 feet wide. The historian Dyonisius of Halicarnassus described the building in these words: "It is surrounded on the south by three rows of columns and

16

OF JUPITER CAPITOLINUS

two rows on the sides." From the high basement rose thirty fluted Corinthian columns, each about 65½ feet in height. The sanctuary was divided into three distinct *cellae,* the central one dedicated to Jupiter Optimus Maximus, the one on the right to Juno, and the one on the left to Minerva. The temple was covered by a single, ridged roof. The cost of just gilding the bronze roof-tiles was, according to Plutarch,* more than 12,000 Attic silver talents, equal to about 38,000,000 gold francs. The Opera House in Paris cost only 36,000,000 gold francs. Moreover, in those ancient days money could buy much more than it can today. Because of its dazzling splendor the Romans called the Capitol *Aureum Capitolium fulgens* (the golden and shining Capitol).

To the left of this great temple were the altar of the Gens Julia and the Temple of Jupiter Custos (Guardian) and to the right was the house of the priests of Jupiter *(Flamines Diales* or *Domus Flaminia)* and the hut of Romulus *(Casa Romuli)* which, according to legend, he occupied when he founded Rome.

* *Plutarch,* by Dacier, 1811. Vol. II, page 158, note 47.

17

INTERIOR OF THE TEMPLE OF JUPITER CAPITOLINU,

A MEDAL OF VESPASIAN'S time shows the front façade of the Temple of the Capitoline Jupiter, with a façade of six columns, as seen in the Restoration, and the three Capitoline divinities, Jupiter Optimus Maximus seated, with the helmeted* Minerva, the Guardian, standing at the left, and Juno the Queen at the right. The central part of the temple was divided into three *cellae*. The middle *cella*, larger and richer than the lateral ones, was consecrated to Jupiter Optimus Maximus, father of all the gods, the greatest divinity of Roman paganism.

The colossal statue of Jove, seated on his throne (see the Restoration) was made of gold and ivory, known as chryselephantine. The statue was copied from the famous Olympian Zeus of Phidias, deemed one of the seven wonders of the world and described by the great historian Pausanias as follows: The head, arms and breast were of ivory. On his right hand he supported the winged victory on the golden globe, and in the left hand he held the sceptre with the golden eagle. On the golden mantle covering his legs the celestial constellations and the signs of the Zodiac were represented with precious stones: sapphires, rubies, oriental pearls *(margaritae),* diamonds and enamelled flowers. Upon the golden throne the *Horae* (hours), Graces, Amazons, Hercules, Apollo, and Diana were carved in relief.

18

* *Les Colosses,* by E. Lesbazeilles, Paris, 1876. pp. 106-110.

JUPITER TONANS   FORTUNA CAPITOLINA

THE TEMPLE OF JOVE, or Jupiter the Thunderer *(Jupiter Tonans)* built of marble blocks, rose in the middle of the Capitoline way *(medio clivo capitolino)*. It was erected in 22 B.C. by the Emperor Augustus to commemorate his escape from death by lightning in the Spanish war: "Coelo tonantem credimus Jovem" (Horace). Between the capitals of the columns Augustus had placed small bells which, according to Pliny, rang during thunderstorms.

In the interior of the temple was a statue of Jove, the work of Leochares. On the outside were the statues of Castor and Pollux (perhaps those seen today at the top of the flight of steps leading to the Piazza del Campidoglio, or Capitol Plaza).

Jove, the Thunderer, was considered to be the janitor or ostiary *(ostiarius)* of the Capitolian Jove.*

At one side of the Temple of Jupiter Tonans rose the tetrastyle (four-columned) Temple of Fortuna Capitolina; an inscription, still extant in Palestrina (ancient Præneste) reads: "Tu, Fortuna, quae Tarpeio coleris vicina tonanti . . ." (Thou, Oh Fortune, who art worshipped near the Tarpeian Thunderer . . .) The Tarpeian

ARCH OF SCIPIO

Rock was at the S.W. end of the Capitoline Hill and from it criminals sentenced to death were hurled.

These temples were located in the area between the present-day Via del Campidoglio (the ancient *Clivus Capitolinus* or Capitoline Way, of which some vestiges have survived near the side entrance to the modern Capitol), and the Via di Monte Tarpeo, in the vicinity of the Municipal Treasury (Tesoro Comunale), in the same Via del Campidoglio.

The Arch of Scipio, built on the street which ascended to the Capitol, had eight gilded columns, a chariot *(biga),* and two marble basins.**

At the right of the Restoration a corner of the ancient *Tabularium* of Q. Lutatius Catulus (79 B.C.***) is seen. Here archives were deposited. This is today the Campidoglio or Capitol.

* *Rome Ant.,* by Nibby. 1838. 1st Vol., pp. 543-544.   ** Titus Livy, Book XXVII, 3.   *** This Catulus was associated with Marius in the defeat of the Cimbri. He wrote a commentary on his part in the Cimbric War, as well as some poetry. (*The Oxford Companion to Classical Literature,* p. 95)

21

THE TEMPLE OF SATURN, of which, in the Restoration, two columns and the flight of steps are shown, is said to have been built by the Dictator T. Lartius in 253 B.C., or by the Consuls functioning in 257 B.C. It was rebuilt, six columns on the façade *(prostylum hexastylum),* during the reign of Augustus, by Lucius Munatius Plancus, in 41 A.D. Some of the columns, which are still to be seen, are part of a later building erected at a time when architecture had fallen into a state of extreme decadence, perhaps during the reign of Theodosius, in 395 A.D. A shaft of one of these columns has fallen, and the bases are unequal.

The public treasure *(aerarium populi Romani, aerarium Saturni)* was kept in the underground vaults of the temple. The ledgers of revenue and expenditures, as well as those of the registrar, the laws and decrees of the Senate, and the standards and ensigns of the legions were kept among the archives.*

There still survive three magnificent angular columns of the Temple of Vespasian, restored by Septimius Severus in 203 A.D., and the last word of an inscription: "Restituer"; this inscription was still extant in its entirety in the eighth

VESPASIAN AND CONCORDIA

century when it was read by the anonymous native from Einsiedeln, Switzerland.

The Temple of Concordia has completely disappeared. An ancient medal shows its façade, with a hexastyle porch or portico *(pronaos),* and two windows of the *cella.* It served as *Senaculum,* for sessions of the Senate. This temple was a real museum of sculpture and painting. All the masterpieces with which it was filled, are enumerated by Pliny (XXXIV, 4). Among them were four elephants of obsidian and the attributes of the imperial power. The entablature of this temple is to be seen today in the Tabularium. A very fine capital with ram's horns at its corners and a highly decorated base (similar in style to the bases of columns found at the Golden House of Nero) are now in the Capitoline Museum. On the still extant steps of the temple are to be seen evidences of a bronze *caduceus* (staff), the attribute of the Goddess Concordia.

23

* *Forum,* by Thédénat, 1904. p. 115.

ARCH OF TIBERIUS AND ROSTRA OF THE ROMAN FORUM

THE FOUNDATIONS OF THE ARCH OF TIBERIUS are seen between the Via Sacra and the Rostra, below the Temple of Saturn (see View of the Present-day Site). This arch was built in 16 A.D. in honor of Tiberius and Germanicus who, after the glorious reconquest of Germany, had recovered the ensigns lost by Varus when the latter was so disastrously defeated in 10 A.D. and three legions were wiped out.

The *Tribuna Rostrata*, or *Rostra*, from which orators harangued the populace, was embellished with the prows of the warships of Antium (taken at the naval battle of Antium, during the period when the Roman Republic was subduing the revolt in Latium), and with the twelve tables of the law *(lex duodecim tabularum)* mentioned by Diodorus Siculus.

On the right (see the Restoration) was the *Umbilicus Romae* (the ideal center of the city), and the Columna Rostrata (see the Restoration) of Duilius, the celebrated conqueror of the Carthaginian fleet at Milae (Milazzo) in Sicily, in 260 B.C. Duilius realized that the Carthaginians were supreme in naval maneuvers, in which the Romans were sadly inexpert. He, therefore, sought to make conditions for his attack on the Carthaginians as nearly as possible those of land fighting in which

24

the Romans had great experience. He used grappling irons and boarding bridges, and their use resulted in the complete defeat of the Carthaginian fleet.

In the center of the Restoration is shown the burning of the records of the Tax and Revenue Office; perhaps under Trajan (98-117 A.D.) on the very spot where now is the commemorative marble bas-relief showing: the Corinthian hexastyle (six columns on the façade) of the Temple of Vespasian, three columns of which are still standing; the Ionic, hexastyle temple of Saturn (eight of the columns are still standing); the arches of the Basilica Julia; the *Ficus Ruminalis* (sacred fig tree), and the statue of Marsias.

The Emperor Hadrian (117-138 A.D.) showed a similar generosity to that above mentioned when he also burnt all the vouchers of the debts which the citizens had contracted with the fiscus; and, in order to give a greater guaranty to all interested parties, he had the obligations, with the names of the tax payers and the sums owed to the Treasury, publicly burnt in Trajan's Forum. The Emperor Hadrian, in addressing the Senate, said that "he was only the servant of the people." This imperial altruism, unique in the world's history, cost the state treasury nearly 43,000,000 dollars.*

25

* *L'Imperatore Adriano* (Italian translation), by Gregorovius, 1910. pp. 4-48.

THE BASILICA JULIA, like other Roman basilicas, was used as a hall of justice by the judges, and as an exchange by the commercial world of Rome. It was begun by Julius Caesar in 54-46 B.C., and completed by Augustus. The hall had two rows of superimposed arches flanked by Doric and Ionic columns. On the side toward the Via Sacra there is still a Doric capital on the pilaster of a half column fragment.

In the hall of the Basilica Pliny the Younger delivered his famous oration in 113 A.D., which he mentions in a letter addressed to his friend Romanus:* "I pled for Attia Viriola, who laid claim to the paternal estate, before the four reunited Sections of the Tribunal. There were one hundred and eighty *(centum et octoginta)* judges, which is the total of the four reunited Sections of the High Court. A great number of the friends of the contending parties were crowded together on the long

26

ON THE ROMAN FORUM

rows of chairs, and in addition there was an immense multitude of listeners who jammed in around the session room, and the very Tribunal was besieged by the public. From the upper galleries of the Basilica men and women leant down, anxious to hear—which was difficult—and to see—which was easier. Great were the expectations of fathers, daughters and even of mothers-in-law. We have won before two Sections, whilst the other two have pronounced against us. Strange whim of fortune!"

The Tribunals were certainly wooden structures and have, therefore, disappeared completely. The vaults of the hall were embellished with very elegant stucco figures and foliage.**

27

* *Epist.* of Pliny. IV, 33. ** *Notices on Excavations,* by Lanciani, 1883. p. 48; also, *Forum,* by Thédénat, 1904. pp. 151-152.

ON THE LEFT IN THE RESTORATION is seen a part of the Arch of Septimius Severus. Below it was a flight of steps, the *Graecostasis* (graecostadion) where the ambassadors and envoys sent by foreign nations to the Senate were received; then came the *Miliarum Aureum* (golden milestone), a column on which the names of the principal towns were inscribed and their distances, on the great roads radiating from Rome.

Then on a line with these monuments come the Curia, or hall of the Senate, now the Church of S. Hadrian. In its ancient façade are still to be seen the triangular fronton (pediment), the cornice of the brackets, the ornamentation of the stucco, traces of the three windows of ancient times (depicted by Du Pérac in 1574), and, below the modern door (which is on the level of Bonella Street) the walled-up bay of the ancient bronze door which Pope Alexander VII, in 1667, took to S. Giovanni in Laterano. This ancient door was located at the principal entrance of the basilica.*

The little Temple of Janus (of Peace and War) was between the Curia and the Basilica Aemilia. The great Basilica Aemilia (see the Restoration) faced the Basilica Julia across the Forum. It was the most magnificent building in the Forum Romanum. It cost about 1,600,000 dollars to build at a time when this sum had a much greater purchasing power than it would have today. Augustus rebuilt it with double arcades. It was dedicated to his nephews, the two Caesars, Gaius and Lucius. Its exterior was embellished with gilded bronze shields, and columns of violet-colored Phrygian marble (pavonazzetto), enriched its interior. According to Pliny it was one of the most sumptuous monuments of Rome and was divided into three sections: Portici (porticoes), Tabernae (shops) and Basilica (hall of Justice and an Exchange for the merchants**).

On the right of the Basilica Aemilia in the Restoration is seen the Temple of Antoninus and Faustina, now the Church of S. Lorenzo in Miranda, and the Temple of Divus Julius Caesar (Caesareum) erected on the spot where the body of the Dictator Julius Caesar was committed to the flames; in front of this temple was erected the Rostra Julia.

The Roman Forum extends between the two *tribunae rostratae*, i.e. the Rostra Vetera (old rostrum) near the Arch of Severus, and the Rostra Julia, in front of the Temple of Caesar. ("Romanum Forum est ubi nunc Rostra sunt" to quote from Servius.) Along the center of the Forum were placed the beautiful Honorary (commemorative) Columns (see the Restoration).

* *Monum. Accad. Lincei*, Mem. 1882-1883, vol. XI; also *Forum*, by Thédénat, p. 99.
** In *Boll. Commiss. Arch. Comun.*, 1889. Article by G. Gatteschi, p. 116 et seq.

28

PORTICO OF THE BASILICA AEMILIA

A CORNER OF THE PORTICO of the Basilica Aemilia is to be seen on the lower left of the Restoration. In the illustration, showing this part of the Forum as it is today the Doric entablature (1st Order) of the Basilica can be seen on the ground near where formerly stood the sanctuary of Venus Cloacina *(Sacellum Cloacina),* and the *Cloaca Maxima* (drainage canal) reached the Forum, on the Street of Janus *(Via ad Janum).*

Near the Basilica Aemilia and almost in front of the Curia (see also the previous Restoration) was the most celebrated temple of Janus, not to be confused with the Arch of Janus, near the church of San Giorgio in Velabro. The doors of the temple remained open in time of war and were shut in time of peace. This little temple is shown on one of Nero's coins. It was restored by Domitian and was brought to light in 1531 A.D.; its dimensions were noted by the architect Labacco; and later it was demolished by Cardinal du Bellay.

The four façades of this small but very elegant temple symbolized the four seasons. In the interior was a statue of Janus pointing (according to Macrobius) to the number 365 (i.e. the days of the year); twelve small altars were dedicated to the twelve months. Procopius (536 A.D.) relates that during the siege of Rome by Belisarius in the Gothic War, some Romans, remembering the old tradition, attempted to force open the temple's four doors.*

The first month of the year (Januarius) is named for Janus.

* *Forum,* by Thédénat, pp. 71-74.

TEMPLE OF JANUS   ROMAN FORUM

The Temple of Castor and Pollux, three columns of which have survived, was erected in 495 B.C. by the Dictator Aulus Posthumius, in commemoration of the Battle of Lake Regillus. It was said that Castor and Pollux themselves came to tell the Romans that their armies were victorious. The Temple was consecrated by Aulus' son in 485 B.C.

Under Tiberius the structure was restored from its foundations up and consecrated again in 6 A.D.

The Basilica Julia was on one side of the Sacred Way *(Via Sacra)* and the Honorary Columns on the other (see the Restoration; also the preceding Restoration).

At the edge of the *Comitium* which was an open space in front of the Curia, where the Via Argelitana came into the Forum, near the corner of the Basilica Aemilia, stood the Statue of Constantine, the pedestal of which is still extant, with a dedicatory inscription of Memmius Vitrasius Orfitus (356 A.D.).

In front of the Curia (see preceding Restoration) was the Fountain of the Comitium (part of which is shown in the Restoration, lower right hand). The basin of the Fountain is perhaps the one now in front of the Villa Medici (French Academy). In the Comitium there was a canal draining off surplus water.

In the left hand corner of the Restoration is shown a flight of steps which led to the Curia (Roman Senate).

31

HORREA AGRIPPINIANA *(General Stores of Agrippa)*

THE HORREA AGRIPPINIANA was located at the foot of the Palatine Hill which is on the south side of the Forum. The site of this structure, between the Augusteum (Temple of the Divine Augustus)—not to be confused with the Mausoleum of Augustus—and the Church of S. Teodoro is indicated by an inscription (still extant among the ruins of the little *aedicula* shown in the center of the Restoration). The inscription reads: "Negotiantibus Horreorum Agrippinianorum" (to the merchants of the Agrippian Stores).

Among the ruins, traces of a portico can be identified, where were the ground floor shops for the sale of goods, while in the upper story were the stores for grain, oil, wine, wool, Spanish silk, glassware, linen, carpets from Sicily and Africa, spices and Arabian perfumes, timber from the Atlantic regions, Babylonian cloths, gold from Dalmatia and Iberia, crystal, oak wood from Massylia, and Indian ivory*.

32

* *Silvae,* by Statius. Lib. III, pp. 85 et seq. ** *Guida di Ostia,* by Vaglieri, 1914. pp. 4 and 5.

All these goods, unloaded at Ostia, were brought to Rome and distributed to the various Horrea, or stores, of the fourteen city districts**. Commerce was very active and extensive and very well organized.

Upon the Horrea were built the so-called "insulae" (apartment dwellings) with pensile balconies, "maeniana" (now called "mignani" or "mignanelli" in the Roman dialect), structures of brick and wood which caused frequent fires in ancient Rome.

At the top of the Restoration is seen the marble portico of the magnificent Domus Tiberiana which was located in what are now the Farnese Gardens on the Palatine, where M. Bianchini made his interesting excavations (1720-1750); his reliefs and drawings have been preserved.

PERISTYLIUM OF THE PALACE OF THE VESTALS *(Domus Virginea)*

SOMEWHAT TO THE EAST of the Temple of Castor and Pollux was this magnificent *Peristylium,* or inner court, surrounded by columns, erroneously called "Atrium Vestae", of the Palace of the Vestals. It measured about 246 feet in length, from wall to wall, and about 85 feet in width. It was erected by order of Emperor Septimus Severus in 193-211 A.D.

The columns of the first story were of "cipollino" marble; the smaller ones of the second story were of pink, "breccia corallina"; there were 92 columns in all. The ground floor, intermediate story and upper floor comprised a total of 84 rooms —for only seven Vestal Virgins! So vast a palace, however, was needed because each Vestal had to have a great number of attendant maid-servants whose duty it was to care for the sacred fire, symbol of the eternity of Rome, which was kept burning night and day in the Temple of Vesta.*

Beneath the portico were statues of Vestal Virgins erected by recipients of miraculous favors, and between the columns were seats whose brickwork was concealed by a veneer of marble.

In the background the reception hall *(Tablinium)* of the Chief Vestal is seen, with three cells on the right and three on the left, perhaps for the use of the other six Vestals.

In the center of the Peristylium, traces of a curious structure, hexagonal in shape, can be seen, with an inner circle. This was probably a fountain with a jet of water *(aqua saliens).* The inner circle was the core of the jet, and the sectors around it formed eight basins.**

Access by men to the Palace of the Vestals was strictly forbidden.

This great palace was worthy of the high position held by the Vestals whom the Romans considered living divinities.

35

*Forum Romanum, by Thédénat. pp. 85 and 316-333; also *Nuova Descr. Casa d. Vestali,* by Marucchi, 1887; also *Foro Romano,* by De Ruggero. pp. 277-293 (1913). ** *Foro Romano,* by De Ruggero. p. 285.

SACARIUM OF JUTURNA   STATIO AQUARUM

SCALAE ANULARIAE

AN INSCRIPTION FOUND BY G. Boni in 1901 near the Lacus Juturnae (pool of the Nymph Juturna), east of the street skirting the Temple of Castor and Pollux in the Roman Forum, tells us the name of this monumental group: "Genio Stationis Aquarum" (to the Genius of the Water Station). The Statio Aquarum was a small sanatorium where sick people came to pray to be cured by the salutary waters from the fountain of Juturna and by Aesculapius, God of Medicine, whose statues are to be seen in the lower part of the central room. Juturna was the sister of Turnus, King of the Rútili; she was changed into a nymph by Jupiter and became guardian of water sources and springs. The Fons Juturnae dates back to the beginning of Rome (750 B.C.). Fons Juturnae, according to the inscription which can still be deciphered, was a miraculous pool or piscine; it is still extant. The ancient legend has it that the Dioscuri (Castor and Pollux) watered their horses there after announcing the victory of Lake Regillus (498 B.C.) to the Roman populace. The Romans defeated the Latins in this battle in which it was said the

36

Dioscuri themselves appeared. For this reason the Temple of Castor and Pollux was built next to the Fons.

In the central islet stood a marble group representing the Dioscuri (the remains of which are to be seen in the Room of Aesculapius where also evidences of three ancient windows are still to be found). At the right (of the Restoration) is the Shrine of Juturna; there is a still legible inscription reading: "Juturnae Sacrum." At the bottom of the well *(puteus)* the living waters still rise to a height of about 4 feet. They always remain at the level of the waters of the Lacus Juturnae. This salutary water was doled out to the sick by special employees. On the pedestal of the Temple of Constantine (328 A.D.) are engraved the names of the physicians who attended the pool.

All these monuments of the Statio Aquarum, sacred to the Goddess Juturna, are of extraordinary importance in the history of the Pagan cults and the history of Roman medicine. Among the monuments were two marble busts, the Apollo Medicus and the Jupiter Medicus.

37

Bibliogr.: *Forum Rom., by Thédénat,* 1904. pp. 279 et seq.; *Foro Rom.,* by Huelsen, 1905. pp. 134 et seq.; *Nomenclator,* by Huelsen. p. 102; *Not. Scavi.,* by Boni, 1901. pp. 41-144.

FORUM OF AUGUSTUS AND TEMPLE

OF MARS THE AVENGER, 2 B.C.

THE EMPEROR OCTAVIANUS, who later assumed the title of Augustus, decided, at the Battle of Philippi, in which the assassins of Julius Caesar were defeated, to erect a temple to Mars Ultor, as the avenger of the great dictator's death. Begun in 42 B.C. and dedicated in 2 B.C., this marvellous temple was in Corinthian octastyle; that is, it had eight columns on its façade and eight on each side. The magnificent columns (about 57 feet, 7 inches high) are still to be seen in the Arco dei Pantani of the wall of the Forum Augustus, which latter abuts on the Forum of Trajan. These are the three end columns of the right side of the temple. Inside the temple, in the center of the apse of the cella, on a pedestal, stood a colossal statuary group representing Mars and Venus (progenitors of the Gens Julia). Augustus was a grandnephew of Julius Caesar, was adopted by the latter, changed his name of Gaius Octavius to G. Julius Caesar Octavianus. Ovid says: "Stet Venus Ultori juncta" (Venus standing with Mars the Avenger). The sword of Julius Caesar was also kept here. In the ruins of the Hall of Justice which is seen on the left in the Restoration, a colossal marble foot (some 6½ feet in length) was found, which perhaps belonged to a statue of Caesar Avenged (the height of the statue judging by the size of the foot, would have been about 39 feet 5 inches).

Octavianus built the Forum Augustus because the great increase of population and, consequently, of law-suits, made it impossible for the Roman Forum and the Julian Forum to accommodate all the business that had to be carried on. This third Forum, therefore, because of this congestion, was built and opened to the public as quickly as possible.

Two buildings, identical in design, were built, respectively to the right and left of the Temple of Mars: one a Tribunal for the public courts (see above) and the other to accommodate the ceremony of drawing lots for the judges. The great enclosing wall (see the Restoration and also the View of the Present-day Site) was about 105 feet high; these buildings stood close to it. It is still extant and in excellent state of preservation; it served, among other things, to protect the Forum Augustus from the frequent fires that broke out in the neighboring houses which were built of wood and bricks (ad arcendorum incendiorum causam).

In the center of the Forum (the Market Square) stood the Equestrian Statue of Augustus. In the subterranean part (favissae) of the Temple was kept the Military Treasure. To the right and left of the Temple stood respectively, the Arches of Drusus and Germanicus (both were members of the family of Augustus).

Bibl.: *Augustus*, by Suetonius, 29; *Le Forum Rom. et les Forums Impériaux*, by Thédénat, 1904. pp. 184-189; *Not. Scavi e Riv. Capitolium*, by Senator Corrado Ricci, 1926-1931; *Forma Urbis Romae et Nomenclator*, by Huelsen and Kiepert, 1921. p. 91; *Fori Imperiali* (Istituta Naz. Luce, Arti Grafiche, Bergamo, June 1930, tables 3-9), by Rob. Paribeni; *Monum. Ant. Roma e Suburibio*, by Gius. Lugli, new edition, Vol. I, April 1931. pp. 45-54.

INTERIOR OF THE BASILICA OF MAXENTIUS (CONSTANTINE)

MAXENTIUS, THE LAST PAGAN EMPEROR, had his Basilica built facing the Media Via Sacra; the present-day Church of SS. Cosma and Damiano, in back of which in ancient times were the Templum and Forum Pacis, is on one side of the ruins of the Basilica, and the Templum of Venus and Roma stood on the other. Three of the Basilica's lofty arches are still standing (see View of the Present-day Site). The great hall of the Basilica was built in the style of the halls of the great Roman baths. Four columns on the right and four on the left supported the three cross-vaults. This building surpassed in grandeur and magnificence all the basilicas that had been erected in Rome up to that time.

The main entrance was in the smaller side of the structure, facing the Temple of Venus and Roma, with an apse in the back. Constantine, conqueror of Maxentius (312 A.D.), added a second entrance toward the Via Sacra, and a second apse in front of the entrance, so that we see the Basilica of today with two apses.

This Basilica served as a model for various celebrated architects of the 16th century: Bramante; Raphael; the two Sangallos; Michelangelo, etc., in planning the new Basilica of St. Peter. As a matter of fact, in both the Maxentian and Vatican Basilicas the central nave has a width of about ninety feet.

The second column at the right (see the Restoration), measuring about 65 feet, 7 inches in height, including base, shaft and capital, remained in place until 1614 A.D., when Paul V (the Borghese) removed it from the spot where it had stood for sixteen centuries, and had it dragged away by sixty horses to the Piazza Santa Maria Maggiore, where it stands to this day. A print by Du Pérac shows the column still in its original location, in the year 1574 A.D.

The total length of the Basilica Maxentius was about 341 feet. The coffers of the vaults were of white stucco with polychrome decorations and gildings. In the niches, which still remain, was placed exquisite and precious statuary. The pavement, uncovered 1810-1813, was red porphyry, green serpentine, "giallo antico", "pavonazzetto" and "cipollino".** An earthquake, mentioned by Petrarch (1349 A.D.), caused the wonderful vaults to collapse. Fragments of them are still to be seen on the pavement under the large central arch and on the pavement of what was formerly the *Forum Pacis,* behind the Church of SS. Cosma and Damiano.

Forma Urbis, by Lanciani.   ** *Forum,* by Thédénat. pp. 345-348.

PORTICUS MARGARITARIA   SACRED WAY

THE *PORTICUS MARGARITARIA* was identified by M. Lanciani as having been in front of the Basilica Maxentius, between the Sacra Via, about 82 feet wide, and the Arch of Titus, the Nova Via, only about 16 feet wide and the Palace of the Vestals (Domus Virginea). It was a large and luxurious bazaar, about 374 feet in length and about 197 feet wide and in earlier times was occupied by the "margaritarii",* merchants of oriental pearls *(margaritae);* but as the population and luxury increased, all sorts of traders and craftsmen flocked in: goldsmiths *(aurifices),* jewellers *(gemarii),* dressmakers making garments of fabrics of woven gold thread *(auri vestrices,)* carvers, engravers, metal founders, garland makers, dye merchants, dealers in ointments, perfumes, cosmetics, in wind instruments *(tibiarii),* knives *(cultrarii),* fruits and honey, and so forth; public scribes, book sellers *(bibliopolae),* pharmacists *(pharmacopolae),* vendors of ham *(pernarii),* pork dealers *(cerretani* from Cerretum in Umbria), locksmiths, joiners, barbers, etc.*

BASILICA MAXENTIUS (CONSTANTINE)

On the ground floor were the porticos and shops (tabernae); in the inner courts the Horrea; and the upper stories consisted of tall tenement structures (insulae). The foundations of the Portico were about 7 feet, 10 inches thick, to support these high buildings (such as, for instance, the Saepta Julia).

In the background of the Restoration are seen: the Fornix Fabianus and the monuments of the Roman Forum; at the top, the Tabularium and the Round Temple of Romulus, son of Maxentius (310 A.D.). On the right is the tetrastyle (four columned) entrance to the Maxentian Basilica, called also Basilica of Constantine, because of an addition to the building made by him in 312 A.D. Rome had in those days attained its population peak, about 1,200,000, and the zenith of its architectural splendor.

43

* *Ruins*, by Lanciani, 1875. p. 209; also *Foro Romano*, by De Ruggero.

SUMMA SACRA VIA AND CLIVUS PALATINUS IN 310 A.D.

THE SUMMA SACRA Via was the highest part of the Via Sacra. At its most elevated point stands the Arch of Titus, erected to commemorate the divine Titus, after his death in 81 A.D., by his brother Domitian (91-86 A.D.). It was also to commemorate the conquest of Judea and the destruction of Jerusalem. In the interior of the Arch are bas-reliefs showing the triumph of Titus, and the famous candlestick with seven branches, taken from the temple of Jerusalem, described by Flavius Josephus.* In the Middle Ages this structure was called *Arcus Septem Lucernarum* (Arch of the Seven Lamps).

Near the Arch of Titus are still to be seen the foundation of the small *Sacellum Larum* (Little Sanctuary of the Lares—Roman tutelary deities), as it was called by Augustus. It was situated on the Summa Sacra Via, and on its site was found an inscription to the *Lares Publici*.** On the left are still to be seen the flight of steps formerly leading to the Temple of Venus and Roma and the columns of the Temple portico lying on the ground (see View of the Present-day Site). On the right (see the Restoration) was the smaller side of the Porticus Margaritaria, with the names of the various merchants on it, and above the portico the tenements, (insulae) built of brick and timbers with wooden balconies (maeniana). Trajan prohibited the building of insulae higher than seventy Roman feet (about 69 feet), but Gibbons states that this law was often disregarded and that tenements of greater height, due to insufficiency of the walls, often collapsed.

At the corner of the Porticus Margaritaria and the Summa Via Nova (Upper New Street) is still to be seen the pedestal of the Equestrian Statue of Clelia (see below), which the records state stood in the Summa Sacra Via.

In the background of the Restoration, at the end of the Clivus Sacer Palatinus (street leading to the Palatine Hill), is to be seen the magnificent Palace of Domitian (Dómus Flavia or Flavian Palace) which dominated the Forum Palatinus (Palatine Forum). In the View of the Present-day Site (the photo was taken in 1902), the pavement of the Sacra Via is still to be seen in the foreground, although the street itself no longer exists.

44

* *The Jewish War,* by Josephus. Lib. VII, Cap. 5,S.5.   ** *Forum Romanum,* by Thédénat. p. 353.

NEAR THE ARCH OF TITUS are still to be seen some enormous blocks of stone, remains of the foundations of the Temple of Jupiter Stator, a place of worship dating back to the days of Romulus, first King of Rome (753-716 B.C.). The Temple was restored by the Consul Posthumius in 294 B.C. M. Tullio Cicero, whose house on the Palatine Hill was located nearby, convoked the Senate to meet here during his consulate and delivered on this occasion his famous oration against Catiline, which began with the often-quoted words: "Quousque tandem abutere, Catilina, patientia nostra?" (How long, oh, Catiline, wilt thou continue to try our patience?). The temple was destroyed during the great fire in Nero's time and was restored by Domitian when he built the Arch of Titus. It is described by Vitruvius as "hexastyle peripterous" (with six columns on the front façade, and eleven at the sides), and is shown as hexastyle Corinthian in a surviving bas-relief.* A Corinthian capital together with a fragment of a column of the building are still extant.

On the right, in the Restoration, are the insulae (tenements) of the Clivus Capitolinus; on the left is the Porticus Margaritaria and in front of the latter, the Equestrian Statue of Clelia. This Roman maiden, legend has it, was one of the hostages
given the Etruscan King Porsenna of Clusium (modern Chiusi) during the Etruscan war. She escaped by swimming across the Tiber under a shower of arrows, but
was sent back by the Romans; Porsenna then set her free, together with some of
the other hostages. Her heroic exploits were commemorated in this equestrian
statue which was set up on the Sacra Via while she was still living, in 508 B.C.**

Behind the Arch of Titus is to be seen in the Restoration the magnificent Temple
of Venus and Roma built by the architect-emperor P. Aelius Hadrian (117-
138 A.D.).

* *Forum Romanum,* by Thédénat. p. 354.   ** T. Livius, Lib. II. p. 13.

47

TEMPLE OF VENUS AND ROMA

THIS TEMPLE, in which were the sanctuaries of both Venus and Roma, was the largest in the city. The architect-emperor Hadrian removed the Vestibulum of Nero's Golden House, and on the cleared space erected this grandiose edifice (121-138 A.D.). One of Antoninus Pius's medals shows the building's front façade as having ten Corinthian columns. The Temple was about 344½ feet long and about 184 feet wide, exclusive of the flight of seven steps surrounding the structure's base. The Church of the Madeleine in Paris is about 321½ feet long and about 141 feet wide, with an octastyle (eight column) façade. The Roman temple was enclosed by 64 columns in all (about 65 feet 7 inches high) of white Proconnesian marble (from the island of Proconnesos, present-day Marmora) in the Sea of Marmora, opposite Constantinople (later known as Byzantium, and more recently renamed Istanbul by the Turks). The roof was covered with gilded bronze tiles some of which were removed by Pope Honorius I (625-640 A.D.) for the embellishment of the ancient Vatican Basilica, and some by the Eastern Emperor Heraclius (610-641 A.D.) to adorn new buildings in Constantinople.* The apses (still extant) of the sanctuaries, one for each deity, were back to back (that of

48

Venus Felix faced toward the Colosseum, that of Roma Aeterna faced toward the Roman Forum).

We possess two ancient bas-reliefs which show the dekastyle (ten-column) façade of the temple, and the triangular pediment with sculptures illustrating the legends of Venus and Roma: Mars and Venus, ancestors of the Gens Julia; and Acca Laurentia and her husband, Faustulus, the shepherd who saved the lives of the twins, Romulus and Remus; the Ficus Ruminalis (sacred fig tree) and the she-wolf that suckled the twins, Romulus and Remus.

The temple stood in the center of a rectangular space (about 492 feet by about 328 feet) which was enclosed on three sides by porticoes; this *peribolon* consisted of 120 columns (about 32 feet, 10 inches high) of gray and red Egyptian marbles. Their fragments are still strewn on the ground. Also some of the arches of the substructures of the basement, in which the treasure was kept, are still to be seen.

* *Ruins,* by Lanciani, 1897. pp. 167 and 199.   *Lexique de Top. Rom.,* by Homo, 1900. p. 629.
Rome Antique, by Homo, 1920. p. 131.

FLAVIAN AMPHITHEATER

COLOSSAL STATUE OF NERO

TEMPLE OF VENUS AND ROMA

BEFORE HE BUILT THE Temple of Venus and Roma on the site of the Vestibulum of the Golden House of Nero, the architect-emperor Hadrian removed the colossal statue of Nero which the latter had had made of himself, to a location between the Colosseum and the proposed temple. Twenty elephants were needed to move the upright statue: The pedestal base, part of which is still extant, on which the statue was placed, was about 57 feet 4 inches long and about 49 feet 2 inches wide. The statue itself, a standing figure of gilded bronze by the sculptor Zenodorus, measured 120 Roman feet (about 118 feet 1 inch) from head to toe,* while the Statue of Liberty, the tallest in existence at the present time, measures only 111 feet 1 inch (exclusive of the arm holding the torch.) The pedestal plus statue added up to about 154 feet 2 inches. The neighboring Colosseum (Flavian Amphitheater) is only about 162 feet, 5 inches high.

After his death, Nero's statue became the Sun God, topped by a seven-rayed crown; each ray was about 12 feet, 4 inches long (according to the Regionari, the fourth century A.D. city recorders). The emperor L. Aelius Aurelius Commodus (180-192 A.D.), notorious for his cruelties and follies, substituted his own head for that of Nero on the statue. But after Commodus's death (192 A.D.) the statue again became the Sun God, and survived, it is thought, till the eighth century A.D.**

Double flights of steps gave access from the plaza of the Amphitheater to the Temple of Venus and Roma and there are still some remains of the steps to indicate where one of them was situated.

* *Nero,* by Suetonius. 31 ** *Vespasian,* 18, by Suetonius; *Hist. Nat.,* by Pliny, LXXI, 15; also Vita Hadriani, p. 19; Scriptores Hist. Aug. and Vita Commodi. p. 17; also *Lexique de Top. Rom.,* by Homo, 1900. p. 154.

PALATINE HILL   ADONAEA

A MEDAL STRUCK in the reign of Emperor Alexander Severus (222-235 A.D.) shows this monumental Entrance to the Gardens of Adonis (Adonaea), with its three arches and three flights of steps, as well as the Temple of Jupiter Ultor, and the porticoes of the Castra Militum (barracks) of the Palatine garrison.* Severus Alexander converted the Temple of the Helagabalium, of Helagabalus, the criminally insane emperor, into the Temple of Jupiter Ultor (the Avenger), to atone for the outrages committed by the madman against Roman religion by the introduction of new oriental cults prohibited by law. About 300 A.D., in the days of the Emperor Diocletian and Maximianus Jovius Herculeus, Sebastian was the commander of the Palatine Praetorian Guard of the Castra Militum, located at the Gardens of Adonis, the present-day Vigna (vineyard) Barberini. Since he was

52

JUPITER ULTOR   ARCH OF DOMITIAN

a Christian, he was sentenced to death, and died a martyr in front of the Temple of Jupiter ("ante Templum Jovis"), according to the *Acta Martyrum*. A very old tradition has it that the present Church of S. Sebastian, on the Palatine Hill at the Vigna Barberini was built on the very spot where the martyr was done to death.

In the View of the Present-day Site, we see the Clivus Sacer Palatinus (Sacred Ascending Palatine Way), a corner of the Propylaea, and the gate of the present Vigna Barberini, which occupies the place where formerly stood one of the three ancient arches. In April 1918, M. Boni, the eminent archaeologist, uncovered the foundations and entablature of the Arch of Domitian, on the Clivus Sacer Palatinus (see Restoration).

53

* *Boll. Comm., Archaeol. Comm.* Bigot, 1911. fasc. I.

PALACE OF CALIGULA AND TEMPLE OF VICTORIA PALATINA

THE SUMMUS CLIVUS VICTORIAE (Ascending Way of Victory) ends exactly at the Temple of Victory *(Templum Victoriae Palatinae)* of which only the foundations remain. The ancient calendars record the games in honor of the Virgin of Victory *(Victoriae Virgini in Palatino)* as taking place on October 26th. The original altar of the Victory dates back to Evander; according to legend Evander was the son of a Goddess and was said to have settled on the Palatine Hill before the founding of the city. The Temple of Victory was erected by the Consul Lucius Posthumius Megellus in 294 B.C. The "black stone" of Cybele, (an aerolith) from Pessinunt in Galatia, was deposited here temporarily, in 206 B.C. The temple was restored in marble by Augustus. In the excavations made by M. Bianchini, 1725-1728, the columns of giallo antico (yellow and cream-colored marble from Numidia) and the marble entablature were discovered.* This temple is not to be confused with the Victoria Germaniciana which stood near the House of Livia (still standing on the Palatine Hill) where Tiberius's mother is said to have lived after the death of his father. On the foundations of the Temple of the Virgin of Victory, M. Boni discovered, on November 4, 1918, a very fine fragment of the "victoria marmorea."

On the left (in the Restoration) we see the Domus Gaiana (Palace of Caligula), with small windows giving light to the Cryptoporticus where Caligula was said to have been killed on January 24th, 41 A.D. These windows still remain, at least in part, intact.

On the right of the Restoration is the Arch of Domitian already described.

Directly before us we have the Forum Palatini, or Plaza of the Palatine, not to be confused with the Area Palatini, which is on the left at the top of a flight of steps, and is on a level some 16 feet higher up.

55

* *Lexique de Top. Rom.* by Homo, 1900. p. 637; also see *Palatino,* by Cancogni, 1909. pp. 54-58.

PALACE OF TIBERIUS AND MEDIUS CLIVUS VICTORIAE

THIS PART OF THE DOMUS TIBERIANA (14-37 A.D.) (see Palace of Caligula, ante) leaned against the Palatine Hill and formed a rectangular court about 95 feet by about 79 feet. (For exterior of the Domus see preceding Restoration.) M. Lanciani has explained in his *Forma Urbis** the true topographical significance of the passage in Suetonius (*Caligula* 22) reading: "Gaius partem Palatii Forum usque promovit". (Caligula extended a part of the Palatine up to the Forum). Apparently Caligula did this by his addition to the Domus Tieberiana. The Restoration shows the two-story Palace of Tiberius with as many rooms as there were arches; the latter are still extant. The rooms of the second floor intercommunicated by an elegant pensile (overhanging) balcony with a marble *transenna* (lattice); it was supported on arches which in turn were supported on brackets of travertine, a special stone quarried mostly at Tibur (Tivoli), used in Roman

buildings. In the View of the Present-day Site, a fragment of this exquisite transenna is seen; under it are some very fine stucco ornaments.

When Caligula (37-41 A.D.) had the Domus Tiberiana extended up to the ancient Via Nova which ran along the Forum Romanum, he constructed new walls in the court of the Tiberian palace perpendicular to the Medius Clivus Victoriae (which ascended to the Palatine Hill from the Forum); these walls supported vaults. In the View of the Present-Day Site one of these vaults can be seen on the left at the top. The rooms of the Tiberian Palace became cellars in Gaius Caligula's time, and the Clivus Victoriae, which in Tiberius' day traversed the court under the open sky, became a real tunnel *(via tecta fornicata)*, i.e. a covered way with vaults and subterranean chambers.

* *Plan of Ancient Rome,* by Lanciani, sheet 29.   ** *Ruins,* by Lanciani, 1897. p. 155.

THIS MAGNIFICENT AULA REGIA (reception-hall-throne-room) was about 138 feet long and nearly 105 feet wide, whereas the central nave of St. Peter's in Vaticano is only 90 feet wide. M. Bianchini's excavations of 1720-26 have given us some details of the building's construction. (There is an inscription by M. Bianchini, 1726, commemorating his notable undertaking.) His excavations showed that there were then on the still extant pedestals sixteen very fine columns of violet-colored Phrygian marble (pavonazzetto) from Phrygia in Asia Minor, with bases and capitals of ivory marble.*

In the niches of this great hall were placed statues of considerable aesthetic value; two of them—Hercules and Bacchus—of black Egyptian basalt, are now in the Royal Museum of Parma. A fragment of the entablature is still to be seen in the Farnese Palace in Rome.

The doorstep, a monolithic block of Grecian marble, about 19 feet 7 inches
long, was used for the great altar of the Panthéon. This type of archaeological
vandalism was committed for the most part in the 18th century.

Every niche in the great hall was flanked by small columns of red Egyptian
porphyry. The pavement was made of red porphyry, green serpentine marble,
giallo antico, and pavonazzetto. The coffers of the vaults, large as those in the
Basilica of Maxentius (also known as the Basilica of Constantine and described
above in this volume) were embellished with large rosettes of gilded stucco. In
the apse of the Aula Regia was the throne (Augustale Solium), where the Eastern
Emperor Heraclius was crowned in 629 A.D. The interior of the Aula Regia
dazzled the beholder with its brilliant polychromy.

* *Ruins,* by Lanciani. p. 159; also *Rovine del Palatino,* by Cancogni, 1909. p. 124.

59

FLAVIAN BASILICA IN THE PALACE OF DOMITIAN

THE FLAVIAN BASILICA was an aula, or private hall, where the Emperor administered justice as head of the state or in legal proceedings of high political and religious importance. There still are extant, as will be seen from the View of the Present-day Site: the apse where the judges presided; *transenna* (open lattices) separating the hemicycle of the apse from the central space reserved for the accused, accusers, lawyers for the defence, witnesses and scribes; a column belonging to the first story of the hall; and the corner walls about 62 feet, 4 inches high, which enables us to determine the height of the ceiling.

This pagan Basilica has served as a model for the Christian Basilica of S. Agnese Fuori le Mura on the Nomentana Road, and S. Antonio, a modern church on the Via Merulana.

This Flavian Basilica is an important landmark in the history of Christendom. The Emperor Domitian (one of the Flavian emperors), avaricious, suspicious and

60

ON THE PALATINE HILL

foe of all virtue, did not spare even those of his closest relatives who had embraced Christianity. It was in this Basilica that he pronounced sentence of death on his own cousin, Flavius Clemens, in 95 A.D.* Clemens' wife, Flavia Domitilla, was exiled to the island of Pandataria (present-day Ventotene). Another Domitilla, niece of the Consul Titus Flavius Clemens mentioned above, was exiled to Ponzia Island.

The discoveries made during the excavations in the cemetery of Flavia Domitilla have established the fact that Christianity had made a number of converts in the Flavian family.**

In the Basilica Flavia the death sentence was also imposed on the renowned St. Sebastian, who suffered a martyr's death in the Castra Militum (Barberini Vineyard of today), about the year 303 of our Lord (see above).

61

* Dion. Cassius, Lib. LXVII, c. 13.   ** *Cimitero di Priscilla,* by O. Marucchi, 1908. p. 50.

TRICLINIUM IN THE DOMITIAN PALACE (Banquet Hall)

THIS MAGNIFICENT TRICLINIUM, a huge hall in which splendid imperial banquets were held (also called the "Jovis Coenatio"), measures about 95 feet by 105 feet. To this hall Martial (*Epigr.* VIII. 39), certainly refers when he remarks: "Before Domitian there was no place on the Palatine worthy of Aulic feasts"; perhaps Juvenal (*Sat.* VII, v. 182-185) also had this Triclinium in mind when he wrote: "a large Coenatio open only to the winter sun, and supported by columns of Numidian marble."

62

The columns of the first story, fragments of which are still to be seen, were of gray Egyptian granite, and those of the second story, of Numidian marble (Numidia was the Roman province known today as Algeria). This summer Triclinium had an open side toward the peristyle (columned portico), i.e. toward the north-east. The two larger sides had windows which looked out on the "Nymphaeums", so that guests could also enjoy looking at the flowers and fountains throwing up jets of water. In the winter all these windows could be closed with panes of glass, and during the winter season hot air circulated under the fine marble pavement which was held up by small pillars of brickwork still extant *(hypocaustum)*. In the central space, between the three great banquet tables *(triclinia)*, Gaditanian dancing girls gyrated, while from the gilded ceiling rose petals rained down on the banqueters luxuriously reclining on the triclinarian couches. In the apse of the hall, reserved for the Emperor, the "terrestrial Jove," the pavement has survived; it is of red porphyry, green serpentine marble, giallo antico, pink breccia corallina, and pavonazzetto.

In this hall the Emperor Pertinax was killed by the Praetorians in 193 A.D.

THE PALATINE AREA was a square on the Germalus (today's Farnese gardens) between the Temple of Jupiter Victor, the House of Tiberius (on the left of the Restoration), the Domus Gaiana or House of Caligula (at the rear of the Restoration), and the Domus Flavia, or House of Domitian (on the right of the Restoration). The Area must not be confused with the Forum Palatini which was on a lower level and which was located between the House of Domitian, the Sacred Palatine Hill, the Temple of the Virgin Victoria and the Area Palatina.

The number of the columns in the Tiberian Portico (on the left in the Restoration) is determined by the still extant windows which gave light to the Cryptoporticus where Caligula is said by some authorities to have been murdered in January, 41 A.D. After committing the crime the assassins escaped (as Josephus Flavius tells us) through the House of Germanicus, now known as the House of Livia, the only house of its kind to have survived to the present day. This house was embellished with some admirable paintings, famous in ancient times. The House of Livia and Germanicus was Tiberius' paternal home, that is to say, it belonged to Tiberius Claudius Nero, father of Tiberius the Emperor and first husband of Livia. Later in 38 B.C. she became the second wife of the Emperor Octavianus Augustus. Augustus is said to have forced Tiberius Claudius Nero to divorce Livia, and he himself divorced his wife Scribonia, so that he could marry Livia. At that time the beautiful Livia was barely nineteen years old. The house later passed to Germanicus, father of Caligula and nephew and adoptive son of Tiberius.

In 10 A.D. the chief of the Germanic tribes, Arminius, exterminated the three Roman legions of Quintilius Varus. But in 14 A.D. Germanicus's military expedition to Germany was launched and two years later the Roman commander defeated Arminius near the River Weser, and won back the Roman Eagles abandoned by Varus. He brought them to Rome as trophies and they were placed on the Palatine Hill. Near the House of Livia and Germanicus stood the Victory Germanicana (a statue of gilded bronze) and nearby was the Vicus (street) Victoriae.

Tiberius reigned from 14 to 37 A.D., and Gaius Caligula from 37 to 41 A.D.

The bases of the columns in the Portico of Domitian (on the right of the Restoration) are still extant. The first Mundus (hut) of Romulus (751 B.C.) stood, according to Josephus Flavius, in the Area Palatina and would probably be found under the Tiberian Cryptoporticus already mentioned, near the corner of this structure that touched the House of Livia.

Bibliogr. *Lex. de Top. Rom.,* by Homo, 1900. p. 61; *Ant. Jud.,* by Josephus Flavius, XIX, 3,1; *Palatino,* by Cancogni, 1909. pp. 80 et seq.; *Le donne dei Cesari,* by G. Ferrero, 1925. p. 31 et seq.; *Germania,* by Tacitus, Paris, 1824, p. 254; *Forma Urbis,* by Lanciani. Sh. 29.

TEMPLE OF JUPITER VICTOR AND HOUSE OF THE FLAMINES

THE FOUNDATIONS, STILL EXTANT, of the Temple of Jupiter Victor (Jove the Conqueror), date back, perhaps, to 294 B.C., when the temple was built by the Consuls Lucius Posthumius Megellus and M. Attilius Regulus to celebrate Roman victories in Samnium, Abruzzo Citeriore, and Etruria, and the conquest of Bolsena, Perugia and Arezzo. Under the Empire the temple was restored in marble, in octastyle peripteral (surrounded by columns), with eight columns in the front façade and thirteen on the sides.* Fragments of these fluted marble columns and a Corinthian capital are still to be seen; from their dimensions it is calculated that the building's columns were nearly 46 feet in height.

Adjoining the temple was the House of the Flamines of Jupiter, or Schola Collegii, the residence of the priestood, which was as imposing as those of the Quindecemviri, the Arvalian Brothers and other similar religious corporations.

We have the register of the elections *(fasti cooptationum)*, relating to the priesthood under Emperor Commodus, of 190 B.C.

It is possible to trace the outlines of the House of the Flamines of Jupiter, which was located between the House of Livia and the Temple of Jupiter Victor. It measured about 111½ feet by 114½ feet and contained the vestibulum, the sleeping quarters (cubicula), atrium, the schola collegii, the assembly hall, kitchen, triclinium (dining hall), etc.

In front of the Temple of Jupiter Victor are to be seen (View of the Present-day Site) the remains of a monumental flight of steps, and on the fourth landing, the remains of an altar.

67

* *Ruins,* by Lanciani, 1897. pp. 138, 139; also *Palatino,* by Cancogni. pp. 132 and seq.

UNDER THE REPUBLIC THE Temple of Cybele, great Mother of the Gods, *(Magna Mater Deum)* was the most important temple on the Palatine Hill and the most active center of religious life. It dates back to 191 B.C. The famous "black stone" (aerolite or meteor) dropped from the sky at Pessinunt in Galatia in Asia Minor, was kept in this temple.* It was transferred to Rome in 204 B.C., during the Second Punic War when Hannibal was threatening Rome with destruction. This black stone symbolized the mother of all the Gods, Cybele, who was portrayed with a tower on her head, standing in a chariot drawn by lions.

The temple was destroyed by fire in 3 A.D. and restored by Augustus, not in marble, however, like the other temples in Rome, but in "peperino" (volcanic tuff containing fragments of various stones and minerals found in the Alban Hills near Rome) with a white stucco coating, i.e. in its original style of Republican architecture. Fragments of fluted columns, shafts, capitals, the cornice, the upper part of the triangular pediment, etc., still survive. In The View of the Present-day Site are shown the stylobate (pavement on which the columns of the temple were supported), near the trees, the headless statue of Cybele, the claws of the lions, the remains of the monumental flight of steps leading to the temple and the stylobate of the small Sacrarium of Juno Sospita (Deliveress) which Ovid mentions as being next to the Temple of Cybele.

The Restoration shows the Emperor Heligabalus, aged seventeen (220 A.D.), as High Priest of Cybele (Archigallus). He was a depraved young man cursed with most unspeakable vices. He is dressed after the oriental fashion of Attis (a Phrygian God worshipped in conjunction with Cybele), standing on a jewel-studded chariot *(biga gemmata)* drawn by four of the most beautiful women ("et quartarnas pulcherrimas mulieres junxit").** In the background, on the right, is seen the portico of the House of Tiberius (also known as the House of Caligula).

68

* *Rome Antique,* by Homo, 1920. pp. 33-34.   ** *Vita Heligab.* by Lampridio. 29.

STADIUM MEGALENSE ON THE PALATINE HILL

THE PALATINE STADIUM may be described as a large court situated between the House of Augustus (see Flavian Palace) on the right, and the Palace of Septimius Severus, the ruins of which are still extant, on the left. The first (ground) floor had Doric columns (see the Restoration) with, between them, arches supported on pilasters and half-columns of stone veneered with marble (breccia corallina rosea). The Stadium was built during Domitian's reign, 95 A.D. The second story had columns with composite capitals and an Imperial Loggia built in the time of Septimius Severus.*

70

Along the wall, on the ground, are still to be seen evidences of the two orders of columns, and the remains of the coffered vaults which were over the first order. The Stadium was nearly 525 feet long and about 157½ feet wide, and is said to have served as a private imperial *Palestra* (wrestling arena) where gymnastic and

athletic spectacles, foot races and discobulus matches took place. Also the Ludi (games) Megalense of the Magna Mater (Cybele) are said to have been celebrated in the Stadium, hence the name Stadium Megalense.**

The basins of the two fountains are still to be seen in the court, and the whole central space was circled by a marble canal *(euripus)* to carry off the water.

During the reign of Theodoric, King of the Ostrogoths, 493-526 A.D., a small Hippodrome, elliptical in shape, was built in the southern section, perhaps for horse races. Its remains can still be seen (see The View of the Present-day Site). Stamped bricks were discovered here bearing the inscription: "Theodoricus Rex pro bono Romae" (King Theodoric for the benefit of Rome).

* *Ruins,* by Lanciani. pp. 174-180; also *Rome Antique,* by Homo, 1920. pp. 50, 51. ** Some archeologists are of the opinion that the Stadium was not used for the purposes here stated, but was an extensive garden.

CIRCUS MAXIMUS, THE CARCERES SIDE
(The Charioteer "Dens" or Stalls)

THE NAME OF THE MODERN STREET, Via Cerchi, which bounds one side of the ancient Circus Maximus, is a somewhat garbled version of "circus." The Via runs the full length of the Circus that backed up against the Palatine Hill. The Circus was about 656 yards long, more than three times the length of the Colosseum which was about 203 yards long. The total width of the Circus was about 295 yards, while St. Peter's is about 212 yards, or, if its portico is included, a few inches more than 230 yards long. The Circus was about 138 feet high; seventy-two tiers of seats on the right, seventy-two on the left, and twenty-six in the curve at the end, accommodated a total number of 135,000 spectators. It was the largest circus (or Hippodrome) not only in Rome but also in the whole empire, and with a greater seating capacity than any stadium of today in the United States. The largest American stadium, the Los Angeles Memorial Colosseum seats only 105,000 persons.

In the center of the Arena was the Spina (a sort of low dividing wall) about 364 yards long; and on it there were some thirty-three monuments and two obelisks. The larger of the two now stands in the Piazza di S. Giovanni, in front of the Basilica of S. Giovanni in Laterano. This obelisk was originally from Egypt and placed by Emperor Constantine in the Circus Maximus in 357 A.D., whence

it was removed to its present location by Pope Sixtus V (about 1587). It is the largest obelisk known to have survived. The smaller of the two obelisks, placed in the Circus by Augustus, was removed to the Piazza del Popolo, by the same Pope.

Races were run in the Arena by bigae (two-horse chariots), trigae (three-horse chariots) and quadrigae (four-horse chariots). There were four factions of the Circus which contended for the palm of victory: the albata (whites), the russata (reds), the prásina (greens) and the véneta (blues); they took their names from the colors they wore. Twelve charioteers, each tied to his chariot, drove out of twelve *carceres* (literally, "prisons" but actually stalls for the chariots and drivers) to take part in the race which consisted of seven circuits of the Spina. The chariot that first passed the posts at the first metae or goals, in front of the carceres, carried off the palm of victory and the fabulous sums that were bet. The original Circus Maximus was bounded on the north and south sides by two streets. The present Via Cerchi (Vicus Consinius) was on one side and another street, found beneath the Jewish Cemetery at the foot of the Aventine Hill, on the other.

Under the Empire, to meet the demands of a growing population, the area of the Circus was doubled by building new walls and adding tiers of seats supported by these walls. The two streets already mentioned were covered over and the new tiers of seats, one tier backing up against the Palatine Hill and the other on the Aventine Hill side, were placed on the roofs bridging the streets. The streets had *fornices* (arched vaults).

Under the Church of S. Anastasia (see View of the Present-day Site, at the left) are still to be seen the enormous and grandiose arches, about 8 feet 2 inches thick, of the Circus Maximus.

There were two great Imperial Loggia, or boxes, the Pulvinar of Augustus and the Pulvinar of Septimius Severus, to accommodate the imperial spectators and their guests.

73

PULVINAR OF AUGUSTUS IN THE CIRCUS MAXIMUS

THE PULVINAR OR IMPERIAL LOGE, for the Emperor and his court, was located near the Podium or low wall which surrounded the Arena, somewhat like the barrier enclosing a Spanish bull ring. The first Pulvinar in the Circus Maximus was built by Augustus, perhaps the same year that he brought the Obelisk from Egypt and placed it on the Spina, in 27 B.C. In the Circus of Romulus (the son of Maxentius), which is still to be seen near the Via Appia, the pulvinar was in front of the meta, or goal, at the "finish"—the most important point in the chariot races.

Behind the pulvinar of Augustus was a magnificent palace for the accommodation of the Emperor and his court, known as the "Kathisma," a Greek term which was also used for a similar building in the Constantinople Hippodrome. Since the races went on for a number of days, the Kathisma was indispensable as a place of rest and recreation. It contained dining-rooms, kitchen, baths, reception hall, atrium, a vestibulum for the body-guard *(Germani Corporis Custodes),* a marble peristyle and so forth. Three arches of the three large halls (at the extreme

rear of the Kathisma) have survived, in the former Loreti premises, on the Via dei Cerchi. In the Tablinium (one of the three halls), murals were uncovered during the excavations of 1892, with life-size figures representing servants *(dapiferi)* bringing food to the tables.*

The pulvinar and tablinium together, have a width of about 49 yards. Between the pulvinar and the podium a space was reserved for the Senators, humble servants of the omnipotent Emperor. Below the podium, on the Arena level, was the euripus, a canal, about 9 feet 9 inches deep and 9 feet 9 inches wide, circling the Arena; it brought water into and carried water out of the Circus.**

The upper portico of the Circus was made of wood, with tiers of wooden seats. This type of construction was the cause of the many accidents, for, apparently, the portico was apt to collapse under the weight of the spectators. In one of these catastrophes, during the reign of Antoninus Pius, there were a thousand one hundred casualties; and in another, in Diocletian's time, thirteen thousand.

* *Notizie Scavi*, 1892. pp. 44.   ** *Moeurs Rom.*, by Friedlander, 1867. Vol. II, pp. 44, 46 and 47.

WALLS OF SERVIUS   PORTA CAPENA

THE ANCIENT PORTA CAPENA, starting point of the famous Appian Way, was situated near the junction of the modern Via di S. Gregorio and Piazza d. Circo Massimo. Its ruins are still to be seen in the lower gardens of the Church of S. Gregorio at the Celian Hill, with the Palatine Hill to the northwest. The remains of the Porta were discovered by Parker and Gori in 1868 and noted on his plan of the city by Lanciani.* On the left, near the gate, once stood the tomb of Horatia.** She was the sister of the three Horatii brothers, who fought the three Curiatii of Alba Longa for the honor of their respective cities. When the only survivor of the fight, one of the Horatii, returned to Rome, his sister, Horatia,

76

TEMPLE OF HONOR AND VIRTUE

called down a curse upon his head because one of the slain Curiatii had been her lover. Horatius thereupon killed her where she stood. Corneille has immortalized this legend in his play *Horace*.

Also on the left was the Temple of Tempests, erected by the Consul L. Cornelius Scipio in 259 B.C.*** On the right, near the gate (see the Restoration) was the Ara (Altar) of Fortuna Reducis, erected (24-19 B.C.) in honor of the Emperor Augustus when he returned from Spain. The commemorative inscription is now in the Royal Museum at Naples.

The most magnificent of all the monuments near the Porta Capena was the Temple of Honor and Virtue, founded in 233 B.C. by the Consul Quintus Fabius

Maximus, the Delayer *(Cunctator)*, whose tactics were responsible for Hannibal's eventual defeat. The temple was restored by the Emperor Vespasian in 70-79 A.D. There were many works of art in this building, and they have been described by Cicero, Pliny and Plutarch. On the fourth of August, 57 B.C., the Senate met in solemn session here to recall Cicero from exile and proclaim him the Redeemer and Father of the Country. When Cicero arrived at the Porta Capena he was welcomed at the Temple steps by a vast multitude which amidst enthusiastic acclamations, accompanied the great orator to the Capitol.

Symmachus states that the Temple actually consisted of two separate sanctuaries, parallel to each other and connected, and with two pediments and two arae (altars), the latter on the flight of steps leading into the buildings. These twin temples were still standing in the fourth century of our era; they had, it seems likely, nine columns on the front façade.***

A small mediaeval tower, the so-called "Passeggiata (promenade) Archeologica," approximately marks the position of the Porta Capena and can be seen in The View of the Present-day Site (in the left hand photograph).

Two aqueducts, the Aqua Marcia and the Aqua Appia passed over the Porta Capena in ancient times.

* *Forma Urbis*, sheet 35.   ** Livy, 1, 26, 2.   *** *Fast,* of Ovid, VI, 193.   **** *Giornale d'Italia,* Article by G. Gatteschi. August 20, 1909.

VIA APPIA OUT OF PORTA CAPENA

THE VIA APPIA, a highroad running from Rome to Campania and lower Italy, was built in 312 B.C. by the Consul Appius Claudius Caccus. Originally it only went as far as Capua, but was successively prolonged to Beneventum, Venusia, Tarantum and Brundisium. Probably it was extended as far as Beneventum not long after the colonization of this town in 268 B.C. Horace, on his journey to Brundisium, described* the Via Appia as far as Beneventum, but not beyond. The original road was, no doubt, only gravelled *(glares strata)*; in 298 B.C. a footpath was laid, *saxo quadrata* (rectangular slabs of stone) from the Porta Capena, by which the road left Rome, to the Temple of Mars, about a mile from the gate. Three years later, however, the whole road was paved with silex (a silicate material) from the Temple to Bovillae, and in 191 B.C. the first mile from the gate to the Temple was similarly treated.

For the first few miles the road was flanked by an unbroken series of tombs and other buildings.** The last section, from Tarentum to Brundisium, was restored by Constantine, c. 315 A.D. In all, from Rome to Brundisium, on the Adriatic side of the heel of the Italian boot, the Via was more than 350 miles long.

The Via Appia was the most famous of Roman roads. Statius*** calls it "longarum regina viarum" (the queen of long-distance roads). It was over this road that St. Paul entered Rome.**** At Brundisium are still extant the two columns that marked the road's terminus.

78

* *Sat.,* by Horace, i, 5 and subs.   ** *Via Appia,* by Canina, Rome, 1853.   *** *Silvae,* by Statius, ii, 2, 12.   **** *Acts,* XXVIII.

FORUM BOARIUM   TEMPLE OF FORTUNA

ARA MAXIMA   ROUND TEMPLE

THE FORUM BOARIUM (cattle market) near the Tiber, and roughly speaking, between the Capitoline Hill to the northeast and the Palatine to the southeast, dated back to the earliest times, and was supposed to mark the spot where, according to the Virgilian legend, Hercules succeeded in recovering his oxen stolen by Cacus.*

On the left of the Restoration is the Temple of Fortune (later the Church of S. Maria Egiziaca). It was, in 1923, freed of its mediaeval additions and conservatively restored.** The Temple was founded by Servius Tullius, one of the Roman kings and restored in 212 B.C., under the republic, by the Consuls Q. Flavius Flaccus and Appius Claudius Pulcher. It is the only republican temple still practically intact, in our times.

The building has columns of the Ionic order, and is about 65½ feet long and about 39½ feet wide. It is built on a stylobate (base) about 8 feet 2 inches thick. The wall of the cella and the columns on the sides are of tufa (a volcanic rock easily worked), covered with a stucco veneer, whilst the columns of the front portico *(pronaos)* and the elegant entablature are of travertine.

In the background of the Restoration is the Arch of Janus Quadrifons, so-

called because of its four façades, still extant in the little square in front of the Church of S. Giorgio in Velabro. It was erected, possibly, by Constantine (313-337 A.D.).

The Ara (altar) Maxima of Hercules (the present-day Pantanella Factory), was built near the Temple of Hercules, as tradition has it, by King Evander, leg--endary figure in Roman mythology who settled on the banks of the Tiber where Rome now stands. It was erected to celebrate the victory of Hercules over Cacus, a monster or brigand, who ravaged the region between the Tiber and the Palatine.*** In the time of the Empire the Ara Maxima was restored in marble. During the papacy of Sixtus IV (1471-1484), a fine statue of Hercules, made of gilded bronze (see the Restoration, right foreground), was found here. The statue is now in the Museum of the Conservatori. On the extreme right center of the Restoration is to be seen the Triumphal Arch of the Circus Maximus. At center of the Forum Boarium we see, in the Restoration, a Bull of gilded bronze mentioned by Tacitus and Ovid, and to the right, the famous Round Temple, erroneously called the Temple of Vesta which was, perhaps, dedicated to Mater Matuta (a female counterpart of Janus and a protectress of childbirth)**** and the God Fortunus. The foundations of this temple belong to the Republican epoch, while the twenty Corinthian marble columns and the marble cella are of the Imperial era. In the middle ages the little Church of S. Maria del Sole was in this temple. In 1813 the seven large steps and the fourteen smaller ones of the stylobate were discovered.

The View of the Present-day Site shows the Temple of Fortune as it was before it was restored.

* *Mitologia,* by Ramorino, 1908. p. 291; also *Ruins,* by Lanciani. p. 515. ** *Encyc. Britannica,* Vol. 19. p. 471. *** *Lex. de Top. Rom.,* by Homo. 1900. **** *Oxford Companion to Classical Literature.*

THEATER OF MARCELLUS   FORUM HOLITORIUM   HERB ELEPHANT

THE THEATER OF MARCELLUS was begun by Julius Caesar and completed by Augustus in 13 B.C., who named it for his nephew Marcellus, son of his sister Octavia. The theater had a seating capacity of 13,000. Today only the first Doric order and the second Ionic order of columns are preserved; the third Corinthian order has been completely destroyed. The Farnese Palace was built in part with materials taken—in the then customary spirit of unscrupulous vandalism—from the Theater of Marcellus, by Paul III (the Farnese pope, 1534-1549). The Savelli-Orsini Palace was built on the ruins of the theater.* Facing the Tiber are some surviving ruins of the theater's scena or stage, which was wantonly destroyed by Sixtus V (1585-1590). These ruins are in the Via di Monte Savello near the gate of the Orsini Palace.**

Via del Teatro di Marcello and Piazza Montanara today occupy the site of the ancient Forum Holitorium which was an herb and vegetable market and, by tradition, there still is a vegetable market there.

On the left (see the Restoration) stood the Columna Lactaria (milk column) where illegitimate infants were brought to drink free milk, provided by the State.*** "Ingenuum infantem in Foro Holitorio triumphum clamasse."**** Festus speaks of a poor baby found at the column "ad quem infantes lacte alendos deferebant."

On the right (see the Restoration) is to be seen the Porticus Frumentaria, or granary, in which by provision of the law of Clodius, corn was dispensed gratuitously to poor families.*****

Two travertine pillars with Doric capitals are still to be seen in the façade of the houses on the right (see View of the Present-day Site).

The fountain of the Herb Elephant (see the Restoration), of gilded bronze, took its name from the Herb Market, and was still extant in 1122 A.D. There is still a fountain there.

* *Rome Ant.*, by Homo, 1920. p. 216.   ** *Topogr. Roma Ant.*, by Borsari, 1897. p. 272.   *** *L'arte di Juno Lucina in Roma,* by G. E. Curatulo, Rome, 1901. pp. 66-67.   **** Livy, XXI, 62. ***** *Lex. de Top. Rom.,* by Homo, 1900. p. 443.

PORTICO OF OCTAVIA AND THEATER OF MARCELLUS

THE AREA OCCUPIED by the famous Portico of Octavia is situated, in modern Rome, between the Via di Pescheria, Piazza Campitelli, the Theater of Marcellus and the Theater of Balbus (Monte Cenci). Here, in 147 B.C., Quintus Caecilius Metellus had a temple erected, dedicated to Jupiter, which was surrounded by porticoes within which the Temple of Juno was included.

These porticoes and Temples were completely restored by Emperor Augustus in honor of his sister Octavia, in 32 B.C. The restoration was directed by the Lacedemonian architect Sauros Batrachos who caused a lizard and a frog to be sculptured on the capitals of the columns of the porticoes, perpetuating his own name thereby, for "Sauros" is Greek for lizard and "batrachos" for frog. One of these columns is still extant in the Church of S. Lorenzo Fuori le Mura (outside the walls). The temples and porticoes, damaged during the fire of 80 A.D., were restored c.203 A.D. by Septimius Severus and Caracalla, who placed the inscription, still to be seen, on the present-day propylaea (entrance gate) in which the Church of S. Angelo in Pescheria was built in the eighth century. In this church, from 1584 down to the era of Pius IX, Jews were forced to come every Saturday and listen to sermons preached by Catholic prelates.

The Temple of Jupiter, perhaps Jupiter Stator, was built by the Greek architect, Hermodorus, but is not to be confused, however, with the other Temple of Jupiter Stator in the Sacra Via Summa. It was the first marble temple erected in Rome.

The Temple of Juno Regina was dedicated by the Censor M. Aemilius Lepidus in 179 B.C. Of this temple there remains a part of its basement and the door of the cella; the latter can be seen in the cellar of the house in the Via S. Angelo di Pescheria; and an impressive and elegant column still stands *in situ*. In this vicinity also was found the pedestal of the statue of Cornelia, mother of the Gracchi, which is now in the Capitoline Museum.

A great number of works of art embellished the Porticoes of Octavia and the two temples; one of them, a Greek masterpiece, is today in the Galleria degli Uffizi in Florence, where it is known as the Venus dei Medici.*

At the corners of the porticoes were pavilions, one of which was identified, in 1867, near the Theater of Marcellus.

In the background (see the Restoration) looms the Temple of Jupiter Capitolinus (in the Palazzo Caffarelli area), and the "cage of the Capitoline geese" which the Romans kept on the Tarpeian Rock in memory of the geese that saved the Capitol when the Gauls attempted to scale it (390 B.C.).

84

* *Rome Ant.*, by Homo. p. 220.

ISLAND OF THE TIBER AND TEMPLE OF AESCULAPIUS

IN 327 B.C. A TERRIBLE PLAGUE caused the Romans to consult the Sybilline books for help. The city fathers were told they could only end the dire scourge if they sent an embassy to Epidauros in Greece to bring back alive the snake, "sacred to Aesculapius," which dwelt there. This was accordingly done. But when the ship carrying the holy reptile reached the Island of the Tiber, the serpent escaped and took refuge in the island. On this spot the Temple of Aesculapius, God of Medicine, was thereupon erected.* To commemorate the prodigy that had occurred there, the island was reshaped to represent the ship which had brought the snake from Epidauros to Rome,** with its prow turned upstream into the current (toward the Ponte Garibaldi of today); so it seemed to people on the banks of the Tiber, who saw the prow dividing the river into two arms, as if a ship were sailing toward them. The poop of the ship was where the Morgue for the bodies of persons who have been drowned, was later built. Still to be seen are remains of the ancient ornamentation, such as the profile of Aesculapius, the

Caduceus (staff) with the sacred snakes, the ox-head *(bucrania),* the travertine brackets, etc., all of which are shown in one of Piranesi's prints.

The masts of the ship were simulated by a cypress tree and an obelisk. On the right and left of the temple were rooms for the sick; this was really a hospital, and there still is a hospital on the Island, the foundations of which date back to very early times.

The Church of S. Bartolomeo all'Isola was built about the year 1000 A.D. on the foundations of the Temple of Aesculapius. The statue of Aesculapius is now in the Royal Museum at Naples.

On the right (see both the Restoration and the View of the Present-day Site) was the Pons Fabricius, which is still intact; it was built in 192 B.C., and was restored by Augustus in 21 B.C. and is today called Ponte Quattro Capi, from the four-headed Hermae on the balustrades (the bridge is also known as the Ponte Fabricio). On the left (see both the Restoration and the View of the Present-day Site), was the Pons Cestius, built of stone by Lucius Cestius in 46 B.C., during Julius Caesar's dictatorship, restored by Emperor Gratian in 365 A.D., and, in 1886-1889, rebuilt in violation of every canon of art and architecture, by modern aediles. The illustration showing the View of the Present-day Site was taken from an old photograph and shows the bridge as it formerly was.

* *Metamorph,* by Ovidius, XV. 622-744.   ** *Lexique de Top. Rom.,* by Homo. p. 312.

TRAJAN'S FORUM AND SERAPAEUM QUIRINALE

TO MAKE ROOM for the magnificent buildings (Forum, Basilica and Column) projected by the Emperor Trajan, the eminent architect Apollodorus of Damascus had to cut away a part of the Quirinal Hill; the section of the hill which he removed ran to a height of some 141 feet, as high as the still extant column of Trajan. The excavated section separated the Forum Augusti from Region VII, the Via Lata, of ancient Rome.*

The Trajan forum proper was an impressive plaza, some 394 feet long, and 377 feet wide. It had two hemicycles (semi-circular recesses), one on each of the long sides of the plaza. These hemicycles were flanked at each end by small apses. Around three sides of the plaza ran porticoes of columns; the portico on the S.E. side had one order of columns; the porticoes on the N.E. and the S.W. sides each had two. The columns were made of precious marbles: giallo antico and rosso antico.

The apse of the great Basilica Ulpia at the N.W. end of the plaza occupied a site on which today stands the Palazzo Roccagiovine. The area between the Basilica

88

Ulpia and the side where the inscription by Pius VII is, enclosed by the wall, scarcely constitutes one-third of the ancient Forum Trajanum.

Behind the houses, toward the Via di Campo Carleo, in a garden, still can be seen the large hemicycle forming a substructure of the Quirinal Hill. On the right, in the Via di Campo Carleo is the other small apse, shaped like the one just referred to.

On the hill, where the Palazzo of the Fondo Culto stands, in ancient times, rose the Serapaeum Quirinale, a magnificent temple consecrated as a shrine of the Egyptian God, Serapis, by the Emperor Caracalla (211-217 A.D.). A colossál capital, Egyptian in style, from this temple, rolled down from the summit of the hill to the Arco dei Pantani (which became one of the entrances to the Forum Augusti), where it was found in 1777. An inscription relating to Serapis was discovered under the Church of S. Agata dei Goti (St. Agatha of the Goths) in the Via Mazzarino.

Trajan was one of the best of the Roman emperors; and was conqueror of Dacia (modern Roumania). Dante praised him in his *Divine Comedy* and there is a legend that Pope Gregory the Great by his prayers obtained Trajan's release from Purgatory. Trajan reigned from 98 A.D. to 117 A.D.**

89

* *Rome Ant.*, by Homo, 1920. p. 154 et seq.; also *Ruins,* by Lanciani. p. 512 et seq.   **Cronologia Storica di Roma,* by Rolando, 1899. pp. 188-195.

THE BASILICA ULPIA served a double purpose: it was both a Hall of Justice and an Exchange for merchants. It was built by the gifted architect Apollodorus of Damascus by command of the Emperor M. Ulpius Trajanus. The large beams of the roof were covered with gilded bronze.*

The columns of the 1st order (see the Restoration) in the great hall, of which fragments are still extant, were of gray Egyptian granite; the marvellous frieze, with "putti," "crateri" and "meandri" (various types of ornamentations), is now in the Lateran Museum. The fragments of the columns and entablatures of the 2nd order are still *in situ*, with fluted columns of giallo antico, pink breccia corallina and Phrygian pavonazzetto. The Basilica Ostiensis of St. Paul (S. Paolo fuori le Mura) was built (396-400 A.D.) over the tomb of the Apostle St. Paul, as a sort of replica of the Basilica Ulpia which then was still standing in all its grandeur. The old Basilica of S. Paolo was destroyed by fire in the early 19th century but rebuilt on the old lines and on the same site. It is interesting to compare the respective dimensions of these two monuments. Each had five naves, the central one about 82 feet wide.

Length of St. Paul's (with apse)	c. 423 feet
Total length of the Basilica Ulpia	c. 607 feet
Width of St. Paul's (5 naves)	c. 203 feet, 5 inches
Width of the Basilica Ulpia (5 naves)	c. 196 feet, 10 inches
Height of St. Paul's	c. 131 feet, 3 inches
Height of the Basilica Ulpia (According to Guadet and Lanciani)	c. 137 feet, 10 inches
Height of Trajan's Column (still standing)	c. 141 feet

The great apse of the Ulpian Basilica (the Hall of Justice) where the judges held court, was located in the area where the present-day Palazzo Roccagiovine stands. In this hall the ceremony of the emancipation of slaves also took place, and it was in this hall that Sidonius Apollinaris, the poet, son-in-law of the Emperor Avitus, recited his panegyric of the Emperor Anthemius (437 A.D.); later Apollinaris was honored by a statue in Trajan's Forum nearby. The fragments of the columns shown in the View of the Present-day Site were part of the Basilica Ulpia, and did not belong to the Forum proper.

* *Description of Greece,* by Pausanias. Italian translation by Nibby, 1834, Vol. 2, p. 163 and Vol. 3, p. 286.

TEMPLE OF TRAJAN   COLUMN   LIBRARIES   BASILICA ULPIA

THE MARVELLOUS COLUMN OF TRAJAN, about 141 feet high, was erected in the small Court of the Libraries, behind the Basilica Ulpia, not in the forum proper. It celebrated the conquest of Dacia (modern Roumania) (101-107 A.D.). It was dedicated in 113 A.D. Trajan's ashes were deposited in a golden urn which was placed beneath the column in 117 A.D.* The column was exactly the height of the Quirinal Hill as it was before Trajan's time. On the column's pedestal is an inscription which reads: "ad declarandum quantae altitudinis mons et locus, tantis operibus sit egestus" (to show how much of the height of the hill and the location have been removed for these great works—*egere,* meaning to carry off, remove). The sepulchral chamber, reached by a small vestibule, was explored by the eminent archaeologist Giacomo Boni in 1906; vestiges were found** of a stone table on which the Urn containing Trajan's ashes was kept.

The column stood in the center of a small court bounded by four buildings: the Basilica Ulpia; the Latin Library; the Greek Library, and the Temple of Trajan. This magnificent temple was built by the architect-Emperor Hadrian (117-138

A.D.) as a shrine to Trajan and his wife Plotina, both of whom had been exalted to the status of deities. The temple was located where the Royal Prefetture (Palazzo Valentini) and the Provveditorato agli Studi now stand between the present-day Churches of S. Nome di Maria and S. Maria di Loreto. It was octastyle peripteral, i.e. with eight columns along the front façade, and fourteen along the sides.***

The two libraries were adjacent to the Basilica Ulpia, to the right and left of Trajan's column, and in front of each of them was a hexastyle (six-columned) portico; vestiges of these porticoes are still to be seen *in situ*.

These splendid structures in the Trajan Forum area were more magnificent than any in the other Imperial Fora; Emperor Constantine when he came from Constantinople on his first visit to Rome in 356 A.D.**** expressed great wonder at and admiration for their grandeur.

93

* *Rome Antique,* by Homo, 1920. p. 158.   ** *Rome Antique,* by Homo, 1920. p. 159.   *** *Forma Urbis,* by S. Lanciani, sheet 22.   **** *Amm. Marc.* XVI. ch. 60.

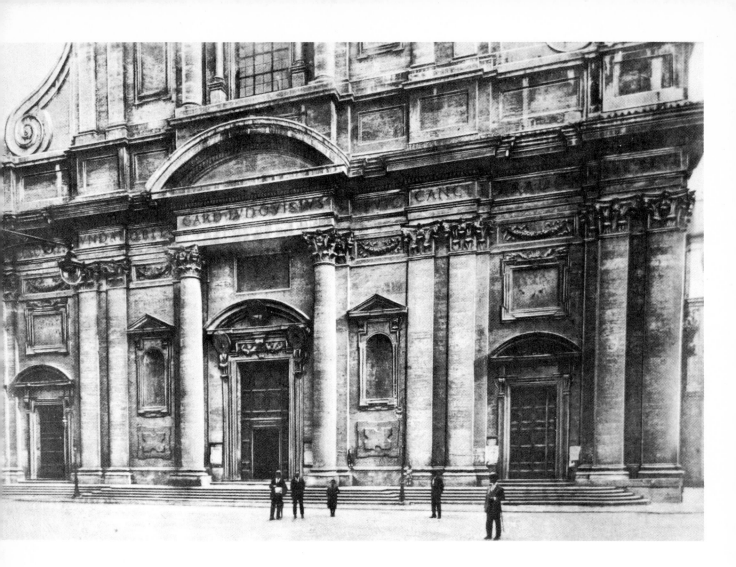

WATER-CASTLE OF THE AQUA VIRGO

IN THE CAMPUS MARTIUS in the N.W. section of Rome there used to be in ancient times, a real Egyptian quarter with a considerable Egyptian colony. Its approximate boundaries were the Saepta Julia (Palazzo Doria—Oratorio del Caravita), Porta Triumphalis (Piazza Grazioli), Serapaeum (Church of S. Marta), Isaeum Campense (Via S. Ignazio) and the Aqueduct of the Aqua Virgo.

The monumental entrance to the Egyptian Quarter was the Castello (water gate) of the Aqua Virgo. This structure was located where the façade of the Church of S. Ignazio now rises.* The columns, pilasters and entablatures of this magnificent building were discovered in 1626 and the discovery was made known to the public by the Jesuit Donati in his *De Urbe Roma,* 1st edition, 1630, Lib. III.** The aqueduct of the Aqua Virgo carried water from east of Rome, in the Via Collatina (*tenuta,* or farm, di Salone). It took its name from the fact that the springs were found by a young maiden (*virgo*) who showed them to some soldiers.

The aqueduct was built by Agrippa to supply his Thermae behind the Panthéon

94

ENTRANCE TO THE EGYPTIAN QUARTER

with water, and was put into operation by him in 19 B.C. It was restored by
Tiberius in 37 A.D., and again by Claudius in 45 A.D.*** The specus (conduit)
is still to be seen beneath the Villa Medici (French Academy). The first section
of the aqueduct ran under the Roman Campagna and the Pincio (in ancient times
known as the Mons Pincius or *collis hortorum* (hill of the gardens), and then
above ground, carried on arches to the Thermae of Agrippa. A magnificent surviving part of the latter section is still to be seen in the Via del Nazzareno (an
arch with three *fornices,* vaults, with an inscription by Claudius) and additional
arches of the aqueduct were discovered in 1886, in the courtyard of the Palazzo
Sciarra on the Corso, and in the small Piazza of S. Macuto near the front of
the Church of S. Ignazio in 1871. The Aqua Virgo is now known as the Aqua
Trevi because it supplies water to the beautiful Fontana di Trevi.   95

* *Forma Urbis,* by Lanciani, sheet 15.   ** *Itiner. di Roma,* by Pellegrini, 1869. p. 72.   *** *Frontino-
Acque,* by Lanciani. p. 120 et seq.; also *Lex. de Top. Rom.,* by Homo, 1900. p. 30.

WE DO NOT KNOW exactly when the Temple of Isis was built, but it seems to have been designed in the style of the Temple of Horus at Edfou in Egypt. Domitian added splendid embellishments to the structure in 95 A.D. The length of both temples (that of Horus in Edfou and that of Isis in Rome) was about 459 feet, a noteworthy coincidence.

The Temple of Isis occupied a part of the site of the present-day Church of S. Ignazio and the street of the same name, a part of the site of the Collegio Romano, the blind alley of the Minerva, and the Via Pié di Marmo.

The temple was Egyptian in style, with, however, some Roman elements—an entrance arch and a portico with Corinthian columns. In the center of the temple court was the famous Dromos, or double row of sphinxes and lions spouting streams of water. Under the Biblioteca (library), Casanatense, in the courtyard of the former Dominican Convent (now the Ministry of Posts and Telegraphs) and the blind alley of the Minerva, when excavations were made there in the 16th and 17th centuries, there were uncovered a number of sphinxes, lions, *canopi*, monkies ("cacchi" and "macacchi"), Egyptian obelisks and two very beautiful statues representing the Nile and Tiber rivers respectively. These two fine works of

art are still extant: the Nile statue is in the Vatican Museum *(Braccio Nuovo)*, and that of the Tiber in the Museum of the Louvre in Paris.

At the Fountain of S. Bernardo (usually known as Fontana dell'Acqua Felice), near the Thermae of Diocletian, are four replicas of Egyptian lions from the temple, the originals of which are in the Vatican. Six of the obelisks are now located in the following places: one in the Boboli Gardens in Florence; one in the plaza of the central railroad station of Rome (this Obelisk is part of the Dogali Monument); one in the Villa Celimontana dei Mattei, also in Rome (this obelisk was presented by the Roman State to Ciriaco Mattei in 1582); one in the Piazza della Minerva, Rome (behind the Pantheon); one in the Piazza of the Pantheon; one in Urbino.

When Egypt was made a Roman province by the Emperor Augustus in 27 B.C., Egyptians came to Rome, established a colony there and built three Egyptian temples as sanctuaries of Isis and Serapis; meanwhile a Roman colony was established in Alexandria and built there its own Roman temples. By this wise policy of religious tolerance the Roman Empire secured to itself the loyalty of the conquered peoples.

TRIUMPHAL GATE OF THE PORTICUS DIVORUM   MONUMENTAL

THIS TRIUMPHAL GATE of the Porticus Divorum is not to be confused with the other two gates with similar designations, of the Quartiere Trionfale and the Wall of Servius. This gate occupied the site of the present-day Piazza Grazioli. It was a monumental entrance to the Porticus Divorum, or portico of the deified emperors, also known as "Porticus Triumphalis," which was located where the Via degli Astalli, Palazzo Grazioli, etc. are today. Josephus Flavius, when he describes the triumph of Titus in 70 A.D. says that Vespasian, Titus and Domitian spent the night near the Temple of Isis and that the triumphal procession formed at the Triumphal Gate.*

A monumental Egyptian fountain, embellished with the model of a ship at its central point, and four Egyptian lions, occupied the site of the old Palazzo della Questura (police department) and was about 82 feet in diameter, like the one in the Piazza Termini. Behind the fountain was the small tetrastyle (four columns on the façade) Temple of Vespasian which is not to be confused with the hexastyle (six columns on the façade) Temple of Vespasian at the Roman Forum. In the imperial era the twelve Arval Brothers, an order of priests performing ceremonies

98

FOUNTAIN   ENTRANCE TO THE SERAPAEUM CAMPENSE

with a view to propitiating the Gods who presided over agricultural activities, frequently held their meetings and sacred *agapes* in this temple.** Legend attributes the name of this order to the following event: the famous courtesan Acca Laurentia, nicknamed "La Lupa," was the mother of twelve sons; when one of them died she adopted Romulus in his place and nursed him. He used to call his brothers by adoption Arval Brothers—brothers of the field (*arva* means field). The order, a sacred college of twelve priests, bore as their insignia a wreath of sheaves and white bands about the head.***

Lastly, on the right (of the Restoration) is to be seen the tetrastyle (four Egyptian columns on its facade) of the entrance to the Serapaeum Campense, and this structure occupied the site on which formerly stood the Church of S. Marta.

The layout of these monuments is indicated in the *Forma Urbis* of Severus,**** about 205 A.D. (Plan of the City). A marble fragment found in the Roman Forum is now in the Palace of the Conservatori in Rome.

99

* *The Jewish War,* by Josephus Flavius, VIII, 5 and 4.   ** *Acta Fratrum Arvalium,* by Marini and Henzen.   *** *Attic Nights,* by Aulus Gellius, VI, 7.   **** *Mitteil. Inst.,* by Huelsen, 1903. p. 17 et seq.

INTERIOR OF THE SERAPAEUM CAMPENSE

THE EGYPTIAN TEMPLE OF SERAPIS in the Campus Martius occupied the site of the present-day Church of S. Stefano del Cacco and part of the site of the former Palazzo Questura, on the Piazza del Collegio Romano. It extended to the modern Via Pié di Marmo, up to the Isaeum Campense (Temple of Isis). The Temples of Isis and Serapis were connected but not united as one place of worship. In front of the temple of Serapis were a large, semicircular pool, and a semicircular portico, as is indicated on the *Forma Urbis* (plan of the city) of Severus, already mentioned.* There was also a large, rectangular court (where was to be seen an inscription: "Serapaeum"), nearly 68 yards long and about 24 yards wide. On the 2nd of September, 1903, in the Via Pié di Marmo, a column of gray Egyptian granite, with bas-reliefs of Egyptian figures and the lotus flower, was discovered. The Church of S. Stefano del Cacco derives its name from a sculptured

cacco or macacco—an Egyptian monkey—found near the church, together with two "Egyptian lions" which are now in the Capitoline Museum.

Serapis was worshipped as the God of the Nether World *(inferi)*, like Pluto; as a symbol of Egyptian fertility, with a *modius* (a basket, or corn measure) on his head; and as a dead bull (Serapis: *Ser*, dead, and *Apis*, bull). Apis was an Egyptian deity assimilated to Osiris who was murdered by his evil brother Set, and so came to be regarded as the God of the Dead, but also as the source of renewed life. The Marble Colossus of Serapis was copied from the Serapis of Alexandria in Egypt, with the modius on his head, and thus portrayed, he symbolized Egypt itself, the granary of the Roman Empire.

The Pié di Marmo (marble foot) from which the name of the street derives, belonged to the Colossus of Serapis. This statue was nearly 26 feet 3 inches high.

* *Mitteil. Inst.,* by Huelsen, 1903. Sheet 17.

101

EXTERIOR OF THE CURIA OF POMPEY   TEMPLES OF

WHEN YOU GO DOWN the Corso Vittorio Emmanuele, toward the Tiber, at the Largo Argentina you face the new excavations of 1926-1931.

The first, rectangular ruin, near the Corso, is perhaps all that remains of the Temple of Minerva Chalchidica, mentioned by Pliny,* and not to be confused with the Temple of Minerva Campense in the Campo Marzio *(Campus Martius)* from which the church known as S. Maria della Minerva derives its name. The Temple of Minerva referred to here was rebuilt by Pompey the Great about 52 B.C. Near it were the Porticoes of Pompey (see the following Restoration). One wing of the porticoes, rebuilt by the Emperor Maximianus Herculeus, in 301 A.D., was called the Hercules Portico.

In the Temple was placed the memorable inscription describing the "thirty years war" waged to a victorious conclusion by Pompey (82-52 B.C.). Of this war it

HERCULES CUSTOS, MINERVA CALCHIDICA

is recorded that "2,183,000 men were defeated, put to flight or taken as hostages, 846 ships captured or sunk, 1,538 towns and fortresses taken, and all the countries from the Palus Moeotis or Sea of Azov, to the Erytrean or Red Sea were subjugated and annexed to the Roman Empire."** A drawing by the architect Antonio da San Gallo, done in the 16th century, shows six Doric columns of the façade of the temple and three on the left side, and one of the cella still standing.

In the courtyard of the house, No. 56, on the Piazza San Nicola ai Cesarini, still stand five fluted columns of the round Temple of Hercules Custos (Guardian); this temple dated back to the time of the Roman Kings, and was restored by the Dictator Sylla about 82 B.C.

Lastly, on the left (of the Restoration of the Exterior), is seen the Curia of Pompey*** where Julius Caesar was murdered on the Ides of March (15th of March) in 44 B.C. The Curia occupied the site of the houses today located be-

103

tween the Via Florida, the Piazza of Pietro Cossa on the Largo Arenula, the Vicolo S. Elena and the Moroni Guglielmi Palace (see the Topographical Sketch). The houses on the Via Florida are perhaps where once were the flight of steps and the pronaos (porch) of the Curia, which gave entrance to the building; the pronaos was about 85 feet, by about 43 feet, and was similar to that of the Temple of Concordia at the Forum Romanum.**** Inside the Curia there was a hall about 144 feet by 75½ feet in size***** (see the Restoration of the Interior of the Curia). It was on this spot that Julius Caesar was murdered under the very eyes of the Senators, by a band of bloodthirsty conspirators.

Plutarch, in his *Life of Caesar* (Ch. 72) and Suetonius in his *Caesar* (Ch. 80-82), describe this infamous and senseless murder which filled and always will fill every human heart with horror. "The conspirators surrounded him. Wherever he looked he saw only swords ready to strike him. Like a wild beast attacked by hunters, he tried to protect himself from all those hands armed against him, for every one of the conspirators was eager to take part in the murder, as they would have wanted to share in the libations of the sacrifices. Brutus inflicted a

SITE OF CAESAR'S DEATH

terrible wound. When Caesar saw Brutus, whom he had adopted as his own son, approaching with his fatal sword, he covered his head with his toga and gave up, without further resistance, to the steel of his enemies. He was pushed to the pedestal of Pompey's statue, which was spattered with his blood. It seemed as if Pompey himself were gloating over the revenge taken on his rival who was expiring at his feet. He was murdered by the infliction of twenty-three wounds. Some of the conspirators, while aiming so many blows at this one man, wounded each other."

The statue of Pompey was very similar to the one in the Temple of Concord in the Roman Forum, where, on special occasions, the Senate assembled.*****

An authentic and ancient replica of this statue of Pompey is now in the Palazzo Spada (Piazza Capo di Ferro) and was found in the Vicolo Leutari, in 1551.

* Pliny, H. N. VII, 21.   ** Pliny, VII, 27.   *** The present-day site of the Curia of Pompey and the two temples, is located by the Via S. Nicola di Cesarini and the former church of the same name, of which there still are some ruins.   **** *Mélanges d'archéologie et d'histoire,* by Bigot, Vil. XXVIII. p. 225.; also *Piccolo Giornale d'Italia,* 18 & 19 Dec. 1915, Article by Gatteschi. ***** *Mélanges d'archéol. et d'hist.* 1908, Paris.

GARDENS AND PORTICOES OF POMPEY, 55 B.C.

THESE PORTICOES WHICH were located not far from the present-day Campo dei Fiori were built by Pompey the Great, 60-55 B.C., around magnificent gardens embellished with fountains throwing up jets of water *(aquae salientes),* statues and shops displaying all sorts of luxury wares. The Porticoes are shown in the marble map of Severus (203 A.D.) already mentioned above. After being damaged by fires and earthquakes at various times, they were restored with the addition of much oriental marble by the Emperors Diocletian, Jovius and Maximianus Herculeus, 301 A.D.* At that time they were called the Hercules Portico and the Porticus Jovia.

The lovely garden was circled by about 260 columns of granite and Egyptian porphyry, cipollino and giallo antico. The length of these porticoes, on the outside, was about 590 feet 6 inches, the width about 475 feet 8 inches, if the Hekastylon, or Portico of a Hundred Columns, be included with the Porticoes of Pompey. In all, there were some 360 columns. Here was a very pleasant place where not only businessmen, but also light women of the town congregated; Catullus, Propertius, Ovid, Martial, Pliny and others mentioned this latter fact. This *paradeison* or garden was embellished with admirable works of art—marble groups and statues, among which are mentioned those of the "fourteen nations" conquered by Pompey in the thirty years' war, 82-52 B.C.

The Porticoes in ancient times covered a rectangle approximately bounded by the Via dei Chiavari, Via dei Chiodaroli, Via di S. Anna, Via del Teatro Argentina, Via dei Sudario, and a part of the Church of S. Andrea della Valle, in modern Rome.

In 1850 a column of Egyptian granite was discovered under a house in front of the Teatro Argentina, and in 1888 four columns of the Porticoes were found in the Via di Torre Argentina, also in front of the theater. In the halls adjacent to the Porticoes were paintings of high artistic quality; they are described by Pliny. All these works of art added up to a magnificent art museum which was always open to the public free of charge.**

107

* *Rome Ant.,* by Homo. p. 223; also *Forma Urbis,* by Lanciani. Sheet 21.   ** *Piccolo Giornale d'Italia,* 18th and 19th of December, 1915. Article by G. Gatteschi.

EXTERIOR OF THE THEATER OF POMPEY, 52 B.C

THE LARGEST, most sumptuous and oldest of the theaters of ancient Rome was the Theater of Pompey. It was situated between the modern Piazza Campo dei Fiori, the Via dei Giubbonari, Via dei Chiavari, part of the Church of S. Andrea della Valle and the Piazza Biscione. In 1840 important excavations were carried out in this vicinity by the architect Baltard, which brought to light some interesting data concerning the Theater of Pompey.* The diameter of the theater was some 557 feet 9 inches.

The Theater of Pompey and the adjoining Temple of Venus Victrix are shown on the marble map of Severus already mentioned above. Around the exterior of the theater ran three orders or stories of columns: Doric, Ionic (both these orders were topped by arches) and Corinthian (with architraves, the lowest part of the entablature resting on the column itself). In the cornice (at the top of the building) masts were fixed to support the *velarius* (awning) which shaded the spectators from the sun.

Pompey dedicated a temple to victory, the Temple of Venus Victrix. A flight of the temple steps led down into the theater** and was a part of the theater, descending through the center of the Cavea, or pit, where the spectators sat, into

the orchestra. These steps also acended to the pronaos or porch of the temple. Up to the time when Pompey built his theater there had been a prejudice against permanent theaters as being too luxurious, in the decadent Greek style, and therefore Pompey located the temple at the top of the Cavea, making the stone seats serve as steps to the shrine of Venus Victrix, in order to disarm criticism.*** In 1525 an inscription was found which bore the name of Venus Victrix. The substructure of the temple was identified in 1865.****

The Theater of Pompey was restored by Augustus, destroyed by fire under Tiberius, rebuilt by Caligula, again destroyed by fire in 80 A.D., rebuilt by Domitian in 95 A.D., again burnt down in the time of the Emperor Philip, 249 A.D., and Diocletian in 290 A.D., and was for the last time restored by the Emperors Arcadius and Honorius in 395 A.D. Although all forms of pagan worship were abolished and Christianity established as the official religion of the State, all of the Roman theaters continued nevertheless to function; this is a very curious fact.

109

* *Indicaz. Topograph.* by Canina, 1850. pp. 368 et seq.; also *Rome Ant., by Homo,* 1920. p. 222; and *Ruins* and *Forma Urbis,* by Lanciani. ** *Attic Nights,* by Aulus Gellius, Liber, X, I. *** *Encyclopedia Britannica,* Vol. 22, p. 21. **** *Lex. de Topogr. Rom.,* 1900. p. 631.

INTERIOR OF THE THEATER OF POMPEY, SCENA,

THE SCENA OF THE THEATER OF POMPEY consisted of a wall with permanent decorations (a sort of permanent set). It was embellished with a triple order (stories) of columns made of a variety of polychrome marbles: red porphyry, green serpentine, giallo (yellow) antico, etc. The roof, which was decorated with gilded coffers (ornamental sunken panels), not only protected the Scena but also served .as a sort of sounding board to carry the voices of the artists to the Cavea (pit where the spectators sat). The Cavea could accommodate 17,550 spectators. (A wonderful description of an ancient theater is given by Julius Polluce in his book, *Teatri antichi e moderni*—Ancient and Modern Theaters.*) Gladiatorial shows as well as dramas were presented in Pompey's Theater. It was opened by a show in which some 500 lions and 20 elephants were slain for the pleasure of the spectators.** In the ancient theater of Aspendos in Asia Minor and the one in Orange, France, the wall of the Scena, about 105 feet high, is still standing, with some fragments of the three stories of columns and the roof.

In front of the Scena was the *Proscenium* or stage, on which the actors per-

PROSCENIUM, ORCHESTRA

formed, and from which a flight of steps led down into the Orchestra, a semi-circular space for the musicians, chorus and dancers; this arrangement can still be seen in the Theater of Bacchus in Athens; in the orchestra there they danced around an altar sacred to Bacchus, called the *Thymele*. St. Augustine speaks of the "thymelica obscenitas" (thymalic obscenity), referring to the dancing girls covered only by a thin veil which they dropped altogether at a given moment.

The Hercules of gilded bronze, seen in the Restoration, above the central door or *Porta Regia* of the Scena, was found under the Palazzo Pio Righetti (Piazza Biscione), and is now in the Sala Rotonda of the Vatican Museum. The two satyrs, respectively to the right and left of the Porta Regia, were found in 1500 in the small Piazza dei Satiri (Square of the Satyrs), and are now in the court-yard of the Capitoline Museum. Another marble Hercules was taken to Paris (Museum of the Louvre).

111

* *Ed. Ferrario*, 1830; also *Arch.*, by Vitruvius, pub. by Amati, Milan, 1829. pp. 154-157. ** *Ency-clopedia Britannica*, Vol. 22, p. 21.

ANCIENT PLAZA OF THE PANTHEON

THERMAE OF NERO   ARCH OF TRAJAN

THE THERMAE OF NERO were measured and sketched by the celebrated architect Palladio in the decade between 1550 and 1560.* These baths occupied the sites of the present-day houses on the left side of the View of the Present-day Site, to wit: the Palazzo Giustiniani, the Senate, the Church of S. Luigi dei Francesi, the small Piazza Pozzo delle Cornacchie, etc.

There was a great square paved with travertine in front of the Pantheon; it extended up to the present-day Via delle Coppelle. The square had porticoes, reached by steps, on only two sides; some evidences of these were discovered in 1871 near the end of the Via dei Pastini.**

In the approximate center of this magnificent square stood the Arch of Trajan, mentioned by P. S. Bartoli; in the Middle Ages it was known as the Arco della Pietà, or Arch of Pity, because it bore a bas-relief illustrating the well-known legend of Trajan's pity for the widow, sung by Dante (Purgatorio X, 76-93):

> *Io dico di Traiano Imperatore;*
> *ed una vedovella gli era al fianco*
> *di lacrime atteggiata e di dolore . . .*

> *(Trajan I speak of, gloriously portrayed,*
> *and there his horse's rein a widow held*
> *in garb of misery and tears arrayed . . .)*

The story goes that Pope St. Gregory the Great had by his prayers liberated the soul of Trajan from Purgatory because of this best of Emperor's sublime act of justice and pity on behalf of the widow.

When Dante was in Rome in 1300 the Arch was still standing but all traces of it have vanished since then.

113

* *Forma Urbis,* by Lanciani, Sheet 15.   ** *Topog. di Roma Antica,* by Borsari, 1897.   p. 303.

MAUSOLEUM OF AUGUSTUS, 27 B.C.

THE FAMOUS GREEK GEOGRAPHER Strabo has left us a description of the Mausoleum of Augustus (at the present-day Piazza Augusto Imperatore), as he saw it when he came to Rome: "A large hill near the river, on a high, round base of white marble, shaded by evergreen trees up to its summit, on which stood the gilded bronze statue of Augustus; and under the tumulus there were the sepulchral cellae of the Emperor, his relatives and members of his household."* The Mausoleum was erroneously called the "Augusteo," while the real *Augusteum,* erected by Tiberius in 14 A.D. after the death of Augustus, is still extant in the Forum Romanum, in the Vicus Tuscus. The Augusteum was the temple dedicated to the deified Augustus. The Mausoleum was the tomb or sepulcher which Augustus erected during his own lifetime, on designs based on the sepulcher of King Mausolus in Halicarnassus, Asia Minor.

114

Two obelisks, discovered behind the Church of S. Rocco, were placed in front of the Mausoleum; one of them now stands in the Piazza Quirinale (Monte Cavallo), and the other in the Piazza dell'Esquilino. On the square base of the

Mausoleum stood, in addition to "four candelabra" at the corners, statuary representing Menelaus and Patroclus; these are now in Florence, in the Palazzo Pitti, in the small court called della Fama, or dell'Aiace.**

The View of the Present-day Site was taken before the Fascist era during which Mussolini ordered the demolition of the Anfiteatro Corea (famous old concert hall), in order to "restore" the Mausoleum. If you view the vicinity from the nearby Church of S. Carlo al Corso, you will be able to observe how Mussolini's "restoration" differs from Strabo's description. The reticulated wall was to be seen in the Via Ripetta (court of the Palazzo Valdambrini) and in the Via dei Pontefici, No. 57, in a court that no longer exists.*** The funerary urn of Aggripina the Elder, grand-daughter of Augustus and one of Emperor Tiberius's victims, is preserved with its inscriptions in the Museo dei Conservatori on the ground floor (court), at the right.

115

* *Georg.*, by Strabo, V. 3, 8.   ** *Rome Ant.*, by Homo, 1920. p. 191.   *** *Forma Urbis*, by Lanciani, Sheet 8.

NYMPHAEUM OF ALEXANDER SEVERUS, WITH

THE REGIONARIES (of the fourteen regions into which Augustus divided the city), of the fourth century A.D., note in the Registro or File V (Esquiline), two monumental fountains, the Nymphaeum of Alexander Severus, and the Fountains of Orpheus (which have disappeared completely). The Lacus Orphei was located in the Via Selci (also known as Orphen) and on the site of the present-day church of S. Martino ai Monti. The ruins of the Nymphaeum Divi Alexandri are still extant in the gardens of the Piazza Vittorio Emanuele and face the Via Carlo Alberto; they are today unfortunately hidden by masses of ivy and tall trees. The photograph of the "Site" reproduced here was taken c. 1875, when the ruins could still be seen, since they were free of vegetation. The three openings from which the water flowed into an upper basin can still be observed. There was a lower basin, level with the ground, into which water poured, also from three apertures which were flanked by little Tuscan columns, the plinths (square part of the base of a column) of which can be discerned in the photograph of the "Site."

A medal, struck during the reign of Alexander Severus (222-235 A.D.) shows this beautiful Nymphaeum and the monumental Fountain of the Aqua Julia, an aqueduct that was first brought into Rome by Agrippa (33 B.C.) and then by Augustus (4 B.C.). The arches of this Julian aqueduct (which supplied water to the Nymphaeum) are still to be seen in the Piazza Guglielmo Pepe, opposite the Jovinelli Theater; and the Grotto can be seen in the Piazza Vittorio Emanuele,

116

TROPHIES OF MARIUS,   ON THE ESQUILINE

to the right of the Restoration and View of the Present-day Site which are reproduced here. Perhaps Emperor Alexander Severus restored the Julian Aqueduct
when he built the Nymphaeum.

He embellished the Nymphaeum with the famous Marble Trophies, known as
the Trophies of Marius; this statuary was probably a copy of earlier bronze
Trophies. Caius Marius, conqueror of the Teutons and Cimbrians, had a house
on the Monte Esquilino; consequently, in the Middle Ages, these two Trophies
were known as "Cimbrum Marii."*

Sixtus V., in 1590, removed the Trophies from Severus's Nymphaeum and
transferred them to the Campidoglio where they still stand, next to the Dioscuri.
A very rare print by Du Perac (1575) shows the two Trophies in their original
setting in the Nymphaeum; the print was made, of course, before Sixtus V. removed
them.

It would seem appropriate to place copies of the two Trophies in travertine stone
in the ruins of the Nymphaeum in the Piazza Vittorio Emanuele, where they had
remained for more than thirteen and a half centuries, from 233 A.D. till 1590 A.D.

* *Forma Urbis,* by Lanciani. Bibl.: *Lex. de Topogr. Rom.,* by Homo, 1900. pp. 25-27; also *Rome
Antique,* 1920. p. 261.; *Gaz. Archeologique,* 1842. Article by Lenormant; *Nomenclator,* by Huelsen,
1912, III. p. 109; *Vestigia di Roma Antica,* by du Pérac, 1575.

THE PONS AELIUS (the present-day Ponte S. Angelo) was built in 138 A.D. by the architect Detrianus (see the Restoration). The commemorative columns on the bridge, with winged Victories, are shown on one of Hadrian's coins, and in a fresco by Raphael in the Vatican. The magnificent tomb is to be attributed to the genius of the great architect-emperor, Hadrian, who not only designed the structure but supervised its construction as well.*

The sides of the square basement of the tomb exactly face the four cardinal points of the compass, and the fifty-two columns of the cylindrical core or nucleus, rising from the basement, were intended perhaps to signify the fifty-two weeks of the year. These columns were moved to the old Basilica of St. Peter in Vaticano, as appears from a drawing by Sallustio Peruzzi. The enormous bulk of humus, more than 3662 cubic yards, discovered by Borgatti in 1901 under the pavement of the papal apartments, came from the original hill *(tumulus)* of the tomb; on the tumulus, funerary trees, such as evergreens, oaks and cypresses grew. The attic of the tomb (see the Restoration) was decorated by fifty-two peacocks with outspread tails of gilded bronze. The Romans considered the peacock a symbol of death. On the very topmost point of this stupendous monument stood a "colossal quadriga" (four-horse chariot) of gilded bronze (described by Johannes Antiochenus in the sixth century) and not the famous "pine-cone" *(pigna)* which adorned the Thermae (baths) of Agrippa and was found in the present-day Piazza della Pigna and taken to the old Basilica of St. Peter, where Dante saw it in the jubilee year of 1300 A.D.

At the four corners of the "lattices" around the basement of the tomb, were peacocks with folded tails, of gilded bronze; two of them are now in the Cortile della Pigna (Court of the Pine-cone) in the Vatican. At the four corners of the square basement were placed great bronze "groups of men and horses", described by Pietro Mallio (in 1160 A.D.). The inscription and corbels (supporting projections) of Parian marble which embellished the square basement, were barbarously removed in 1579 by Gregory XIII and used to decorate the Gregorian Chapel of St. Peter's.**

In the Middle Ages the tomb became a fortress, known as Castel Sant'Angelo because of the statue of St. Michael at the top of the structure (see View of the Present-day Site); this statue was placed there to commemorate the vision of Pope Gregory the Great in which the archangel told the pope that the plague of 590 A.D. was ending. The Castel became a refuge for the popes in times of emergency.*** The corridor which the popes perhaps used to escape to the castle, is still extant. In this fortress Benvenuto Cellini was held prisoner; and from it he made his daring escape. In this fortress, also, Beatrice Cenci was beheaded, as punishment for the crime of patricide.

* *Castel Sant'Angelo,* by Borgatti. Rome 1911; also *Lex. de Top. Rom.,* by Homo. p. 336.   ** *Destruction de Rome Antique,* by Lanciani, 1905. p. 106.   *** *Rassegna Internationale Roma.* I Luglio, 1902. anno III, vol. X. pp. 36-39, article by G. Gatteschi

CIRCUS OF NERO AND HORTI GAIANI IN VATICANO

NERO BUILT HIS CIRCUS in the Horti Gaiani, or Gardens of the Emperor Gaius Caligula. He built it around the obelisk brought by Caligula from Egypt to Rome.* The carceres (cellars where the performers and victims were confined) of the Neronian Circus covered the sites of the present-day little Churches of S. Marta and S. Stefano dei Mori, and the curve of the Circus reached into a part of the modern Piazza di S. Pietro (in Vaticano). The Circus was some 377 yards, 1 foot long, and about 114 yards, 2¾ feet wide. The point where the obelisk was placed is indicated by an inscription at the Piazza della Sacrestia (Piazza del Circo Neroniano). Pope Sixtus V ordered the architect Dom. Fontana to remove the obelisk to the Piazza S. Pietro in 1586, and there is still stands. At the foot of the obelisk (justa Obeliscum intra duas metas), near the Spina (the low wall running down the center of the arena) in the ancient Circus, St. Peter suffered a martyr's death in 67 A.D., a victim of the first persecution of the Christians by Nero. "The Christians were crucified and their bodies, smeared with resin, were set afire, serving as torches to illuminate the Neronian garden, while Nero, garbed in the costume of an auriga (charioteer) drove a chariot around the Circus."*

The body of the Prince of the Apostles was placed in a tomb on the Via Cornelia that ran along the side of the Circus; this tomb is marked by a cross, in the Restoration. In the fourth century A.D. the Circus of Nero was demolished and above the Sepulcher of St. Peter was erected the "venerable ancient Vatican Basilica" by the Emperor Constantine, in the shape of a Latin cross (313-333 A.D.).**

For twelve centuries the Basilica remained intact, a prototype of a primitive Christian basilica, with all the memorials and relics of the first martyr popes and the first Christian emperors. But in the 16th century it was ruthlessly swept away, a crime of high treason against Christianity, in order to make way for the triumph of pagan-renaissance architecture which the new Basilica of St. Peter illustrated on such a grandiose scale. Ignorance of Christian antiquity and a blind, fanatic aversion to everything classical, considered as contemptible and barbaric the buildings of primitive Christianity.

* Ruins, by Lanciani, 1897. pp. 551 et seq.   ** Annals, by Tacitus, XV, 44.   *** Tib. Alpharani de Antiquissima Basilica Vaticana, by Cerrati. Rome, 1914; also Chiese di Roma, by Armellini, 1891. pp. 727 et seq.

INDEX

THE NUMBERS CORRESPOND TO THOSE ON THE ENDPAPER MAPS.

RESTORATION	VIEW OF THE PRESENT-DAY SITE
Panorama of the Palatine Hill with Roman Forum and surrounding monuments	Palatine Hill, Roman Forum and surrounding monuments
I, AI Exterior of the Temple of Jupiter Capitolinus	Via di Monte Caprino, gardens and former Palazzo Caffarelli, Via di Monte Tarpeo
Interior of the Temple of Jupiter Capitolinus (Colossus of Jupiter in the middle Cella)	
Jupiter Tonans, Fortuna Capitolina, Arch of Scipio	Via del Campidoglio
A4, A5, A6 Clivus Capitolinus, Temples of Saturn, Vespasian and Concordia	Clivus Capitolinus
A7, A3 Arch of Tiberius and Rostra of the Roman Forum	Roman Forum, Rostra, Temples of Saturn and Vespasian
A8 Interior of the Basilica Julia on the Roman Forum	Basilica Julia
A26, A25, A24, A3 Arch of Septimius Severus, Curia, Basilica Aemilia, Roman Forum	Forum, Curia, Basilica Aemilia
A24, A3 Portico of the Basilica Aemilia, Temple of Janus, Roman Forum	Basilica Aemilia and Roman Forum
A12, B2 Horrea Agrippiniana (General Stores of Agrippa)	Horrea at the foot of the Palatine Hill
A14 Peristylium of the Palace of the Vestals	Palace of the Vestals (House of the Vestals)
A10 Sacrarium of Juturna, Statio Aquarum, Scalae Anulariae	Ruins of the Sacrarium of Juturna

RESTORATION	VIEW OF THE PRESENT-DAY SITE
B11 Temple of Jupiter Victor (Propugnator) and House of the Flamines on the Palatine Hill	Foundations of the Temple of Jupiter Victor
B12 Temple of Cybele and Sacrarium of Juno Sospita	Ruins of the Temple of Cybele
B13 Stadium Megalense on the Palatine Hill	Ruins of the Stadium Megalense
B14 Circus Maximus, showing the Carceres (Charioteer dens)	Church of S. Anastasia, Via dei Cerchi
Detail of the Pulvinar (loge) of Augustus in the Circus Maximus	
6, B15 Walls of Servius, Porta Capena, Temple of Honor and Virtue	A Ruins of the Porta Capena at the Passeggiata Archeologica
	B Via Appia at the Porta Capena
7 Forum Boarium, Temple of Fortuna, Ara Maxima, Round Temple	Piazza Bocca della Veritá, Columns of the Temple of Fortune embedded in the Church of S. Maria Egiziaca, Round Temple (so-called Tempio di Vesta)
10, 8 Theater of Marcellus, Forum Holitorium, Herb Elephant	Piazza Montanara and Via del Teatro Marcello
12, 10 Portico of Octavia and Theater of Marcellus	Ruins of the Octavian Portico
9 Island of the Tiber and Temple of Aesculapius	Island of the Tiber (in 1867) Ponte Fabricio and Ponte Cestio before it was rebuilt
A30, 3 Trajan's Forum and Serapaeum Quirinale	Piazza del Foro Traiano
Interior of the Basilica Ulpia (113 A.D.)	Palazzo Roccagiovine showing ruins of the Forum Trajanum
A33, A32, A34, A31 Temple of Trajan, Column, Libraries, Basilica Ulpia	Foro Italico and Colonna Traiana
15, 16, 17, 11 Water Castle of the Aqua Virgo, Entrance to the Egyptian Quarter	Piazza and Church of S. Ignazio

RESTORATION	VIEW OF THE PRESENT-DAY SITE
A20 Interior of the Basilica of Maxentius (Basilica of Constantine)	Maxentian Basilica
A15, A20 Porticus Margaritaria, Sacra Via, Basilica of Maxentius (Constantine)	Summa Sacra Via and Porticus Margaritaria
A16, A17 Summa Sacra Via and Clivus Capitolinus (in 310A.D.)	Steps of the Temple of Venus and Roma, Arch of Titus, Summa Sacra Via (in 1902)
A16, A17 Summa Sacra Via, Arch of Titus, Temple of Jupiter Stator	Arch of Titus and Summa Sacra Via (in 1902)
A18 Temple of Venus and Roma	Temple of Venus and Roma
5, 4, A19, A18 Flavian Amphitheater, Colossal Statue of Nero, Temple of Venus and Roma	Colosseum, Pediment of the Colossal Statue of Nero, Temple of Venus and Roma
B1 The Palatine Hill, Adonaea, Jupiter Ultor, Arch of Domitian	Vigna (vineyard) Barberini, ruins of the Adonaea, Church of S. Sebastiano, ruins of the Clivus Capitolinus
B3, B8 Palace of Caligula and Temple of Victoria Palatina	Area Palatina and runis of the Domus Gaiana (Palace of Caligula)
B4 Palace of Tiberius and Medius Clivus Victoriae	Domus Tiberiana and Medius Clivus of Victory
B9 Aula Regia in the Palace of Domitian	Aula Regia of Domitian
B9 Flavian Basilica (Hall of Justice) in the Domitian Palace	Ruins of the Flavian Basilica
B9 Triclinium (Banquet Hall) in the Domitian Palace	Palatine Hill and ruins of the Triclinium in the Palace of Domitian
B5, B3, B4, B9 Palatine Area, Palaces of Tiberius, Caligula and Domitian	Palatine Area

125

RESTORATION	VIEW OF THE PRESENT-DAY SITE
16, 17 Isaeum Campense or Temple of Isis, in the Campus Martius	Via di S. Ignazio, Collegio Romano
16, 17 Triumphal Gate of the Porticus Divorum, Monumental Fountain, Entrance to the Serapaeum Campense	Piazza of the Collegio Romano, old Questura Palace, Church of S. Marta
Interior of the Serapaeum Campense	Piazzetta and Church of S. Stefano del Cacco
18 Exterior of the Curia of Pompey, Hercules Custos, Minera Calchidica	Piazza and Church of S. Nicola ai Cesarini
Interior of the Curia of Pompey (Site of Caesar's death)	Ruins near the Largo Argentina
	Topographic sketch to indicate the position of the Curia of Pompey
19 Gardens and Porticoes of Pompey (B.C. 55)	Largo Arenula, Via di Torre Argentina, Piazza S. Elena
20 Exterior of the Theater of Pompey (B.C. 52)	Piazza Campo dei Fiori
Interior of the Theater of Pompey, Scena, Prosecenium, Orchestra	
13, 14 Ancient Plaza of the Pantheon, Thermae of Nero, Arch of Trajan	The Modern Piazza del Pantheon
21 Mausoleum of Augustus (B.C. 27)	Anfiteatro Corea (concert hall) before Mussolini's restoration
24 Nymphaeum of Alexander Severus with the trophies of Marius, on the Esquiline	Ruins of the Nymphaeum in the Piazza Vittorio Emanuele (in 1875)
A29 The Forum of of Augustus and the Temple of Mars the Avenger (B.C. 2)	Ruins of the Forum of Augustus (excavations 1926-1931)
22 Tomb of Hadrian and Pons Aelius	Bridge and Castel S. Angelo
23 Circus of Nero and Horti Gaiani in Vaticano	Exterior of the apse of St. Peter's in Vaticano